Caliban and Other Essays

Caliban
and Other Essays

Roberto Fernández Retamar

Translated by Edward Baker
Foreword by Fredric Jameson

University of Minnesota Press
Minneapolis

Published by the University of Minnesota Press
2037 University Avenue Southeast, Minneapolis, MN 55455-3092
Printed in the United States of America on acid-free paper

Second printing, 1994

Library of Congress Cataloging-in-Publication Data

Fernández Retamar, Roberto.
    Caliban and other essays / Roberto Fernández Retamar ; translated by Edward Baker.
        p.   cm.
    Translated from Spanish.
    Bibliography: p.
    Includes index.
        Contents: Caliban—Caliban revisited—Against the black legend—Some theoretical problems of Spanish-American literature—Prologue to Ernesto Cardenal.
    ISBN 0-8166-1742-2
    ISBN 0-8166-1743-0 (pbk.)
        1. Latin America—Civilization. I. Title.
F1408.3 1989
980-dc 19

Contents

Foreword
Fredric Jameson

The English translation of these essays by Roberto Fernández Retamar ought to be the occasion for rethinking the relations between poetry and politics — or even between literary criticism and politics in a situation in which increasingly no one wants to think about that relationship any longer. Not, however, because (as was the situation some thirty years ago, around the time of the Cuban Revolution) it is forbidden to raise "extrinsic," political, social, and historical issues in the same breath with poetic and verbal textures: today virtually everyone acknowledges the deep constitutive interrelationship between poetry and politics, between language and power. No, silence today is generated by the seeming perplexity in the West as to what politics — what *a* politics — might be in the first place: a perplexity no doubt meaningless in the rest of the world — very emphatically including Cuba — where the political is a destiny, where human beings are from the outset condemned to politics, as a result of material want, and of life on the very edge of physical catastrophe, a life that almost always includes human violence as well. The peculiarity of First World life (and of the preoccupations of First World intellectuals) is then the possibility of forgetting, of repressing, the political altogether, at least for a time; of stepping out of the "nightmare of history" into the sealed spaces of a private life about which the most remarkable, singular, historical characteristic is that we have come to forget that its very existence is a historical anomaly, and to regard it as sheerly natural, to imagine that it corresponds to some "human nature," and that its values — the priority of "real" private existential life over public matters — are self-evident and virtually by definition require no defense or examination.

I find, as I knew I would, that I have used an expression—"First World"—that would be repudiated by the author of these essays. My task is, of course, different from his, even though we have a common political and ideological struggle: for I conceive my business to include, at least in part, the effort to sting North American intellectuals (or more precisely, U.S. ones, since we lack the convenient word *estadunidense*) into some sense of our own unique historical situation which is *differential*. Such an awareness—unlike the complacencies of the myth of American or Northamerican exceptionalism—would be accompanied by, and indeed inseparable from, a constant awareness of all those cultural Others with whom we coexist and from whose existence in some peculiar way our own "identity" is derived, when it is not more literally based on those other cultures by way either of derivation or of exploitation. But this differentiality—and I use this ugly word because the word "difference" has become a political and ideological slogan today, most often of an anti-Marxist kind—is by definition pledged to perpetual movement and displacement. Our traditional difference from the Europeans, for example, and even from a Europe now in many ways "americanized," ought to reinforce our cultural solidarity, as a postcolonial nation, with the postcolonial nations of Latin America (of whom Cuba has always been the closest to us in all respects). To use the terms of Fernández Retamar's book, under these circumstances José Martí ought to be a more interesting reader of Emerson for us than Nietzsche. . . . But if that does not turn out to be so, then we witness this provisional constellation of solidarities and differences slowly breaking up and reforming into other ones, in which the obvious fact of our other identity as the bankers, arbiters, exploiters, arms suppliers, and military policemen of Latin America then slowly again come to take precedence.

But Roberto Fernández Retamar has a keener sense of the dialectics of difference and the paradoxical reversals of Identity and Difference, of the Same and the Other, the supremely mutable polemics of marginality and centrality; and it is time to give him the floor. His classic *Caliban* is after all, if anything is, the Latin American equivalent of Said's *Orientalism* (which it preceded by some six or seven years) and generated a similar ferment and restlessness in the Latin American field; while its sustained and passionate eloquence, the deep breath of its polemic vocation, mark it stylistically and formally as a unique moment in the fortunes of that dying form, the modern cultural pamphlet, in which we ourselves have increasingly so little to show (I take it that this is the burden of Russell Jacoby's "pamphlet," *The Last Intellectuals*, which, however, oddly forgets to mention Said himself, or Chomsky, or feminist polemicists, or black ones).

In Jacoby's spirit, then, we can reconstruct from these essays of Roberto Fernández Retamar a certain image and function of the political intellectual which we ourselves have lost. He offers the example of two kinds of identifications which used to define certain intellectuals, even in the West, but which today

seem decisively on the wane, and not only among us either. A poet and an essayist, he still combines the classical intellectual's supreme commitment to language in all its capacities which has been, in late capitalism, systematically un-
dermined by specialization and the ever intensifying social division of labor
(something often more narrowly deplored as the withdrawal of literary critics and
theorists to the university). Meanwhile, as an "esthete"—if one may so charac-
terize the great poetic and visionary vocation of the Poet that survives in Latin
America as in a few other national traditions—his commitment to politics is
equally absolute; or rather—in sharp distinction from the now dominant "tradition" of Anglo-American poetry and modernism—there is felt to be no incon-
sistency between poetry and politics in this alternate tradition. With characteristic
generosity, Fernández Retamar allows this supreme alternate possibility to be
dramatized by the revolutionary poet of another, related, but distinct tradition,
that of Nicaragua and of Ernesto Cardenal. But what Fernández Retamar's own
work in particular and Cuban literature in general can also mean for us is this
exhilarating spectacle of an Art and a Poetry fulfilled by the Revolution, and
finding its very myth and telos of fulfillment in the figure of revolution itself: a
lesson about which the poetry in our own language has at least since Shelley been
phlegmatic and our poetic theory and criticism altogether mute.

Yet a third feature of Fernández Retamar's activity as an intellectual demands
to be mentioned here, since it will also be reflected in the form and content of the
essays that follow: and this is his role as editor of the journal of the Casa de las
Américas (since 1965), and his eventual assumption of the direction of that institution in 1986. To call the Casa de las Américas a publishing house, or, on the
other hand, a cultural center of some sort, is to begin to sense another deeper
lesson of the present essays, namely the unsuitability of our cultural and institu-
tional categories—developed in and for the market system—for the novelty of
socialist institutions (but also for the uniqueness of Cuba's cultural and political
vocations). In film, in literature, in politics, Havana has become something of an
alternate capital of the Americas—but also, and slightly distinct from that, an
alternate capital of the Caribbean world: an alternate possibility that must be kept
alive in the failure of the old dream of a unified Latin America, or of the real-
ization of some newer sense of pan-Caribbean identity. The annual film festival,
the selection of Cuba as the site for the new panamerican film school, the almost
weekly conferences at Casa drawing artists, writers, and intellectuals from all
over the Americas, above all the presitigious prizes in a range of genres offered
by the Casa de las Américas to Latin American and Caribbean writers—these are
in a socialist context and perspective matters a good deal more significant than
"mere" cultural politics or even "propaganda."

In fact, the essays here collected may be read as one long yet multiple meditation on the problem of internationalism itself, and of the possible relationships

to be established between the fact of an uneven global system, on the one hand, and the dual coordinates, on the other, of a socialist collective project and of the inevitably national context of cultural production as such. Cuba has to be sure been uniquely successful in projecting its own multiple national identities (Latin American, Caribbean, African, even North-American) onto its international cultural and political relations. Retamar is here less interested in mapping or evaluating such a politics, however, than in charting the paradoxes and dilemmas of the dialectic of otherness.

Caliban thus famously affirms identification with the voice of the slave in a statement contemporary with other analogous Cuban cultural expressions in literature, Miguel Barnet's *testimonio* of Estaban Montejo, or in film, Sergio Giral's *El Otro Francisco* or Gutierrez Alea's *Last Supper*. Yet what the essay necessarily wrestles with is the vicious rebound programmed into the double bind which is the starting point for such revolt and such affirmation: "Does a Latin American culture exist?" Can you do anything but curse in this alien language? Have you not thereby already recognized the cultural superiority of the colonizer? But the double bind is reversed in the second essay in this collection, in which the "curse" must itself be dismantled, and the "black legend" of the Spanish conquerors as racist and inhuman is itself stigmatized as what is often today called "inverted racism." Not merely the supreme example of Las Casas himself, but also the yankee interest in staging Spain as an inferior mode of production, in which capitalism failed owing to Roman Catholicism and absolute monarchy, and which was thereby unable to endow its colonies with the commercial vitality of the Northern tier—these twin considerations awaken the appropriate suspicions about the ultimate value of *Caliban*'s most instinctive polemic.

The same issues return more subtly in the essay on literary historical problems, where now the "language" and the "export" is literary critical methodology (most notably, in that period, what used to be called structuralism): when one thinks about it, the North American situation has not been terribly different in this respect, except that we have had the time to forget the first shock of our colonization by the waves of properly European methods consumed here avidly since the later 1960s. Even in the other major preoccupation of this essay—the question of whether properly European modes of periodization and the nomenclature of European movements are appropriate to the radical difference of Latin American culture—we in the North have no little stake in the matter, and Fernández Retamar's provisional "solution"—that the more "marginal" cultural areas of Eastern Europe may present more useful analogies to postcolonial literature than the "central" imperial cultures—is a productive and stimulating one. No less relevant, meanwhile, are the considerations on genre, which suggest that Western European forms have often served as a focus that masks the emergence in Latin American of stranger, more calibanesque, less immediately classifiable texts (Fernández Retamar then usefully proposing the "estrangement" offered by the very difference traditions and cultures of some of the Eastern European countries).

In light of such considerations, we may conclude by asking ourselves whether it is any longer appropriate to introduce Roberto Fernández Retamar as a distinguished *Cuban* cultural intellectual (let alone as a Second World one, or even a Third World one). What seems essential to me, and what follows from his own reflections here, is the need to convert the binary and invidious slogan of *difference* into the rather different call for *situation-specificity*, for a positioning that always remains concrete and reflexive. But that kind of historical situational remains for most idealist intellectuals a scandal. In fact the old belle-lettristic quarrel about the intrinsic and the extrinsic was never solved or resolved: it merely migrated to different zones where it reemerges when you least expect it. You are free today to talk as much about Shakespeare's political or economic background as you like; but when you say the word *Ireland* in connection with Yeats or Joyce, then you have pronounced the unmentionable and reminded English Departments about their discomfort with these foreigners: you have remembered a war, and reintroduced *content* into literary study and discussion in an unpardonable way, using your fingers. The word *Cuba* has a very similar scandalous power: literary and cultural criticism can absorb an enormous range of topics (turning them in the process into metaphysics, neutralizing them as sheer philosophy), but the existence of socialism is not one of those, and the apprehension is unpleasant that a radically different social system, alive and well and not very far away from us, and linguistically and socially accessible, might somehow disqualify all our most deeply ingrained professional and intellectual values.

In any case, the new global system demands some new conception of "comparative literature," or of "world literature," as Goethe called it: a need sometimes obscured or blotted out by cultural—including a specifically *theoretical*—imperialism, in which a common canon of Western modernist and theoretical texts seems slowly to cover the world. Goethe's original concept of "world literature" had nothing to do with eternal invariants and timeless forms, but very specifically with literary and cultural journals read across national boundaries and with the emergence of critical networks by which the intellectuals of one country inform themselves about the specific intellectual problems and debates of another. Nor are such boundaries any longer purely national, in the sense of the atlas or gazetteer, as a whole internal third world within the U.S. testifies (Hispanics will be the largest U.S. minority by the year 2000, something which the increased virulence of the bilingualism debates clearly registers).

We, therefore, need a new literary and cultural internationalism which involves risks and dangers, which calls us into question fully as much as it acknowledges the Other, thereby also serving as a more adequate and chastening form of self-knowledge. This "internationalism of the national situations" neither reduces the "Third World" to some homogeneous Other of the West, nor does it vacuously celebrate the "astonishing" pluralism of human cultures: rather, by isolating the common *situation* (capitalism, imperialism, colonialism) shared by very different kinds of societies, it allows their differences to be measured against each other as well as against ourselves. Such a perspective might be expected to introduce class struggle—on a new and global scale—into comparative literature (in the spirit in which Althusser used to recommend that we reveal it as "always-already" at work within the philosophical tradition). The present essays will have been, and very much continue to be, an active component in that process.

Preface

This isn't the first time I've told the story of how I arrived in New York, like Stingo in *Sophie's Choice*, in the summer of 1947. I had finished my secondary studies in Havana, and my parents rewarded my not having done badly (I've always been ashamed to confess that I was first in my class) by sending me "North" for a few months, a not uncommon occurrence those days in Cuba, even for modest *petits bourgeois* like my parents. I went off, my head filled with a welter of books — mainly poetry and essays, socialist writings, avant-garde art criticism. I was drunk on those readings. I had just turned seventeen, and although I had not yet published a single line, I felt certain, and there were others who shared my feeling (I'll be damned if I know why), that I was a poet.

New York won me over little by little. I alternated daytime visits to the Museum of Modern Art and other museums and galleries and walks in the city with nighttime get-togethers with the friends whose life I shared: humble Puerto Ricans. We would meet in a barbershop on 180th Street that belonged to one of them, where I picked up my mail. I identified with that group up to a point: I was just one more poor Puerto Rican in New York. But they were simple people who didn't care for my intellectual leanings and I could not and would not do anything to counter those leanings.

New York was very free in 1947. The war had just ended, and now and again the press published criticisms of North American racism (an utter atrocity for a Cuban like me), which some compared to the anti-Semitism of the recently defeated Nazis. I found that satisfying. Of course, I couldn't imagine that in that very same year, 1947, McCarthyism, which would keep me away from the United

States for ten years and many years after that would lead me to an impassioned reading of Lillian Hellman's *Scoundrel Time,* was taking its first steps. I remember the young men and women in the Columbia University subway station loaded down with books, some of which had the name of Karl Marx emblazoned on their covers. It would be nice (I thought) to study there. But, of course, I had to work for a living.

While that decision was brewing inside me and the date of my departure drew near, I went to the movies one night. They were showing *Odd Man Out.* Although the Irish cause has always moved the great majority of Latin Americans, I barely could pay attention to the movie because of the sign on the box office that said Usher Wanted. What a great job that would be: at night I'd wander the movie house like a shadow, with my flashlight, and during the day I'd be a student, at Columbia University if I could. By the time the movie had ended and I left the theater, anxious to talk to the woman at the box office, they had already taken down the sign. A few days later I left for Cuba.

In the next ten years I worked, studied in my own country and in Europe, participated in a little political activity, published books of poetry and criticism in Cuba and abroad, and made the acquaintance of jail and Greece, linguistics and Paris. I found out, in other words, what it meant to become a university teacher and in one of the classic Latin-American dictatorships propitiated by Washington, a dictatorship that kept my university closed.

In the autumn of 1957 I returned to the United States as a professor at Yale. René Wellek was also teaching at Yale, and he was good enough to read the manuscript of my *Idea de la estilística* [The Idea of Stylistics], as well as to acquaint me with the work of the Prague Linguistic Circle and, in particular, that of Roman Jakobson, who then was at Harvard. At the end of that year Columbia University opened it doors to me, not as a student but rather as a lecturer on ''The Present Situation of Spanish-American poetry,'' which Columbia would publish in its *Revista Hispánica Moderna.* In early 1958 I returned to Cuba and, disgusted at the country's situation and not believing that the tyrant could be overthrown (although my incredulity did not prevent me from working with the resistance movement in a variety of ways, one of which was to write against the dictatorship in a clandestine magazine under the pseudonym of ''David''), I accepted an invitation to teach full-time at Columbia beginning in the spring of 1959. But on the first of that year the rebels led by Fidel Castro succeeded in overthrowing Batista. What joy! I cabled Columbia expressing my feeling of moral obligation to decline the honor of their invitation and stay home, where I would return to my university teaching and become a journalist, diplomat, journal editor, director of institutes, and a thousand other things (to the detriment of linguistics, which would stay with me like an old flame). The essays collected here are among the consequences of that decision.

If I had stayed in New York in 1947, I might be writing in English, like Conrad and Nabokov. Or if the Cuban Revolution had not been victorious in January 1959 and as a result I had gone to teach at Columbia, I might still be there, uprooted and torn apart. But none of that happened. What did happen was that for nearly thirty years my life has been fused with the most important historical event in Latin America since the wars of independence. Moreover, since I was twenty-eight in 1959 and had a certain kind of educational background, had lived abroad, and published books, I necessarily brought some part of the past to the Cuban revolutionary process. I believe I am, as I said in a poem written in 1965—the first copy of which I sent for obvious reasons to Che Guevara—a "transitional man," although at this point the biggest and best part of my life is decidedly on the present and future side of the dividing line. And although I would not at all disdain the many enriching influences of general culture on my work, that best part of my life has been nourished above all by historical reality. Thus, the absolute need to make sense (for myself and for others) of what I was living brought forth many pages, including the ones in this book. On more than one occasion I argue heatedly with a debating partner on whom I cannot always pin a name and who, even when he has another name, is at times myself, the man I used to be.

Of all my essays, the one that has received the most attention and brought me the greatest number of intellectual friendships (as well as polemics) is, without doubt, "Caliban" [Caliban] (1971). As I tried to say fifteen years later, in "Calibán revisitado" [Caliban Revisited], the earlier piece stemmed from a particular, and difficult, situation for my country and myself, and it should be read with that situation in mind. Later on, I tried to write a few companion pieces, but they are barely represented in the present volume, which is necessarily anthological and designed for a North American readership. I scarcely need mention how important that readership is for me. Neither it nor the United States are at all alien to me; if it is not crudely ironic, I should be mindful that *et in Arcadia ego*— And not only myself, whose debt to the best of the United States history and culture is evident, but all of Cuba, which for sixty years, from 1898 to 1958 was, to put it a bit bluntly, part of the empire. Even before the first of those dates, our great man, José Martí, had lived the last fifteen years of his life in the United States, and they were indispensable years for his intellectual development: they made him not only the most advanced of our thinkers but a North American radical as well. When, in January of 1895, he left New York for Cuba (in whose War of Independence against old Spanish colonialism and nascent North American imperialism he would die shortly thereafter), among the portraits that remained in his modest office at 120 Front Street was one of the great abolitionist and member of the First International Wendell Phillips. Martí's relation to North American culture pointed the way for those of us who wish to follow his teachings. Although, on the one hand, he criticized with ever-greater lucidity the ills of North American society and the danger that one sector of it represented for Latin America and the

Caribbean (which Martí always called "our America"), on the other hand, (as Juan Ramón Jiménez stated, thinking of his great essay on Whitman from 1887), "Spain and Spanish America owe him, in large part, our poetic access to the United States."

At the beginning of *Reading Capital*, Louis Althusser assured us that there are no innocent readings.[1] Here, read by a poet and an enthusiast of his revolution, are some literary and cultural matters from the entirety of our America, and from Spain as well. The publishers, wisely, have decided to include a short piece on the poetry of Ernesto Cardenal. I find this satisfying for a number of reasons, and my very great regard for his poetry is not the only one. It permits me to render homage in a very basic way to the event that, twenty years after the victory of the Cuban Revolution, lit the fires of hope in me once more—the Sandinista Revolution. Right now, as I write these words, even more than when I wrote my most recent piece on the great poet of Nicaragua, his country is in grave danger. There, in the birthplace of Rubén Darío, the founder of modern poetry in Spanish; where Augusto César Sandino was born the day before José Martí died in combat and where his guerrillas defeated the North American invaders in the 1920s and 1930s, an admirable people live, dream, build, and fight to construct a more just society according to their own lights. Inevitably, as is usual in this part of the world, their wish has provoked the blind fury of the worst of North American society. Accordingly, I would like to dedicate this volume to the new Nicaragua and, simultaneously, to people of conscience in the United States, who, honoring their noblest traditions, will help check the continuing aggression—taking place under the excuse of the East-West conflict—against the country where our heart is today.

Caliban and Other Essays

Caliban:
Notes Toward a Discussion of
Culture in Our America

A Question

A European journalist, and moreover a leftist, asked me a few days ago, "Does a Latin-American culture exist?" We were discussing, naturally enough, the recent polemic regarding Cuba that ended by confronting, on the one hand, certain bourgeois European intellectuals (or aspirants to that state) with a visible colonialist nostalgia; and on the other, that body of Latin-American writers and artists who reject open or veiled forms of cultural and political colonialism. The question seemed to me to reveal one of the roots of the polemic and, hence, could also be expressed another way: "Do you exist?" For to question our culture is to question our very existence, our human reality itself, and thus to be willing to take a stand in favor of our irremediable colonial condition, since it suggest that we would be but a distorted echo of what occurs elsewhere. This elsewhere is of course the metropolis, the colonizing centers, whose "right wings" have exploited us and whose supposed "left wings" have pretended and continue to pretend to guide us with pious solicitude—in both cases with the assistance of local intermediaries of varying persuasions.

While this fate is to some extent suffered by all countries emerging from colonialism—those countries of ours that enterprising metropolitan intellectuals have ineptly and successively termed *barbarians, peoples of color, underdevel-*

This article appeared for the first time in *Casa de Las Américas* (Havana), 68 (September-October 1971). It is that journal, and that issue specifically, to which the author refers in the text.

oped countries, Third World—I think the phenomenon achieves a singular crudeness with respect to what Martí called "our *mestizo* America." Although the thesis that every man and even every culture is *mestizo* could easily be defended and although this seems especially valid in the case of colonies, it is nevertheless apparent that in both their ethnic and their cultural aspects capitalist countries long ago achieved a relative homogeneity. Almost before our eyes certain readjustments have been made. The white population of the United States (diverse, but of common European origin) exterminated the aboriginal population and thrust the black population aside, thereby affording itself homogeneity in spite of diversity and offering a coherent model that its Nazi disciples attempted to apply even to other European conglomerates—an unforgivable sin that led some members of the bourgeoisie to stigmatize in Hitler what they applauded as a healthy Sunday diversion in westerns and Tarzan films. Those movies proposed to the world— and even to those of us who are kin to the communities under attack and who rejoiced in the evocation of our own extermination—the monstrous racial criteria that have accompanied the United Sates from its beginnings to the genocide in Indochina. Less apparent (and in some cases perhaps less cruel) is the process by which other capitalist countries have also achieved relative racial and cultural homogeneity at the expense of *internal* diversity.

Nor can any necessary relationship be established between *mestizaje* ["racial intermingling, racial mixture"—ed. note] and the colonial world. The latter is highly complex[1] despite basic structural affinities of its parts. It has included countries with well-defined millennial cultures, some of which have suffered (or are presently suffering) direct occupation (India, Vietnam), and others of which have suffered indirect occupation (China). It also comprehends countries with rich cultures but less political homogeneity, which have been subjected to extremely diverse forms of colonialism (the Arab world). There are other peoples, finally, whose fundamental structures were savagely dislocated by the dire activity of the European despite which they continue to preserve a certain ethnic and cultural homogeneity (black Africa). (Indeed, the latter has occurred despite the colonialists' criminal and unsuccessful attempts to prohibit it.) In these countries *mestizaje* naturally exists to a greater or lesser degree, but it is always accidental and always on the fringe of the central line of development.

But within the colonial world there exists a case unique to *the entire planet:* a vast zone for which *mestizaje* is not an accident but rather the essence, the central line: ourselves, "our mestizo America." Martí, with his excellent knowledge of the language, employed this specific adjective as the distinctive sign of our culture—a culture of descendants, both ethnically and culturally speaking, of aborigines, Africans, and Europeans. In his "Letter from Jamaica" (1815), the Liberator, Simón Bolívar, had proclaimed, "We are a small human species: we possess a world encircled by vast seas, new in almost all its arts and sciences." In his message to the Congress of Angostura (1819), he added:

Let us bear in mind that our people is neither European nor North
American, but a composite of Africa and America rather than an
emanation of Europe; for even Spain fails as a European people because
of her African blood, her institutions, and her character. It is impossible
to assign us with any exactitude to a specific human family. The greater
part of the native peoples has been annihilated; the European has
mingled with the American and with the African, and the African has
mingled with the Indian and with the European. Born from the womb of
a common mother, our fathers, different in origin and blood, are
foreigners; all differ visibly in the epidermis, and this dissimilarity
leaves marks of the greatest transcendence.

Even in this century, in a book as confused as the author himself but full of
intuitions (*La raza cósmica,* 1925), the Mexican José Vasconcelos pointed out
that in Latin America a new race was being forged, "made with the treasure of
all previous ones, the final race, the cosmic race."[2]

This singular fact lies at the root of countless misunderstandings. Chinese,
Vietnamese, Korean, Arab, or African cultures may leave the Euro-North American enthusiastic, indifferent, or even depressed. But it would never occur to him
to confuse a Chinese with a Norwegian, or a Bantu with an Italian; nor would it
occur to him to ask whether they exist. Yet, on the other hand, some Latin Americans are taken at times for apprentices, for rough drafts or dull copies of Europeans, including among these latter whites who constitute what Martí called
"European America." In the same way, our entire culture is taken as an appren-
ticeship, a rough draft or a copy of European bourgeois culture ("an emanation
of Europe," as Bolívar said). This last error is more frequent than the the first,
since confusion of a Cuban with an Englishman, or a Guatemalan with a German, tends to be impeded by a certain ethnic tenacity. Here the *rioplatenses* appear to be less ethnically, althogh not culturally, differentiated. The confusion
lies in the root itself, because as descendants of numerous Indian, African, and
European communities, we have only a few languages with which to understand
one another: those of the colonizers. While other colonials or ex-colonials in metropolitan centers speak among themselves in their own language, we Latin Americans continue to use the languages of our colonizers. These are the linguas fran-
cas capable of going beyond the frontiers that neither the aboriginal nor Creole
languages succeed in crossing. Right now as we are discussing, as I am discussing with those colonizers, how else can I do it except in one of their languages,
which is now also *our* language, and with so many of their conceptual tools,
which are now also *our* conceptual tools? This is precisely the extraordinary out-
cry that we read in a work by perhaps the most extraordinary writer of fiction
who ever existed. In *The Tempest,* William Shakespeare's last play, the deformed
Caliban—enslaved, robbed of his island, and trained to speak by Prospero—re-
bukes Prospero thus: "You taught me language, and my profit on't/ Is, I know

how to curse. The red plague rid you/ For learning me your language!''(1. 2.362–64).

Toward the History of Caliban

Caliban is Shakespeare's anagram for "cannibal," an expression that he had already used to mean "anthropophagus," in the third part of *Henry IV* and in *Othello* and that comes in turn from the word *carib*. Before the arrival of the Europeans, whom they resisted heroically, the Carib Indians were the most valiant and warlike inhabitants of the very lands that we occupy today. Their name lives on in the name Caribbean Sea (referred to genially by some as the American Mediterranean, just as if we were to call the Mediterranean the Caribbean of Europe). But the name *carib* in itself—as well as in its deformation, *cannibal*— has been perpetuated in the eyes of Europeans above all as a defamation. It is the term in this sense that Shakespeare takes up and elaborates into a complex symbol. Because of its exceptional importance to us, it will be useful to trace its history in some detail.

In the *Diario de Navegación* [Navigation logbooks] of Columbus there appear the first European accounts of the men who were to occasion the symbol in question. On Sunday, 4 November 1492, less than a month after Columbus arrived on the continent that was to be called America, the following entry was inscribed: "He learned also that far from the place there were men with one eye and others with dogs' muzzles, who ate human beings."[3] On 23 November, this entry: "[the island of Haiti], which they said was very large and that on it lived people who had only one eye and others called cannibals, of whom they seemed to be very afraid." On 11 December it is noted " . . . that *caniba* refers in fact to the people of El Gran Can," which explains the deformation undergone by the name *carib*—also used by Columbus. In the very letter of 15 February 1493, "dated on the caravelle off the island of Canaria" in which Columbus announces to the world his "discovery," he writes: "I have found, then, neither monsters nor news of any, save for one island [Quarives], the second upon entering the Indies, which is populated with people held by everyone on the islands to be very ferocious, and who eat human flesh."[4]

This *carib/cannibal* image contrasts with another one of the American man presented in the writings of Columbus: that of the *Arauaco* of the Greater Antilles—our *Taino* Indian primarily—whom he describes as peaceful, meek, and even timorous and cowardly. Both visions of the American aborigine will circulate vertiginously throughout Europe, each coming to know its own particular development: The Taino will be transformed into the paradisical inhabitant of a utopic world; by 1516 Thomas More will publish his *Utopia*, the similarities of which to the island of Cuba have been indicated, almost to the point of rapture, by Ezequiel Martínez Estrada.[5] The Carib, on the other hand, will become a *cannibal*—an anthropophagus, a bestial man situated on the margins of civilization, who must be opposed to the very death. But there is less of a contradiction than might appear at first glance between the two visions; they constitute, simply, options in the ideological arsenal of a vigorous emerging bourgeoisie. Francisco de Quevedo translated "utopia" as "there is no such place." With respect to these two visions, one might add, "There is no such man." The notion of an Edenic creature comprehends, in more contemporary terms, a working hypothesis for the bourgeois left, and, as such, offers an ideal model of the perfect society free from the constrictions of that feudal world against which the bourgeoisie is in fact struggling. Generally speaking, the utopic vision throws upon these lands projects for political reforms unrealized in the countries of origin. In this sense its line of development is far from extinguished. Indeed, it meets with certain perpetuators—apart from its radical perpetuators, who are the consequential revolutionaries—in the numerous advisers who unflaggingly propose to countries emerging from colonialism magic formulas from the metropolis to solve the grave problems colonialism has left us and which, of course, they have not yet resolved in their own countries. It goes without saying that these proponents of "There is no such place" are irritated by the insolent fact that the place *does* exist and, quite naturally, has all the virtues and defects not of a project but of genuine reality.

As for the vision of the *cannibal,* it corresponds—also in more contemporary terms—to the right wing of that same bourgeoisie. It belongs to the ideological arsenal of politicians of action, those who perform the dirty work in whose fruits the charming dreamers of utopias will equally share. That the Caribs were as Columbus (and, after him, an unending throng of followers) depicted them is about as probably as the existence of one-eyed men, men with dog muzzles or tails, or even the Amazons mentioned by the explorer in pages where Greco-Roman mythology, the medieval bestiary, and the novel of chivalry all play their part. It is a question of the typically degraded vision offered by the colonizer of the man he is colonizing. That we ourselves may have at one time believed in this version only proves to what extent we are infected with the ideology of the enemy. It is typical that we have applied the term *cannibal* not to the extinct aborigine of our isles but, above all, to the African black who appeared in those shameful Tarzan films. For it is the colonizer who brings us together, who reveals the profound similarities existing above and beyond our secondary differences. The colonizer's version explains to us that owing to the Caribs' irremediable bestiality, there was no alternative to their extermination. What it does not explain is why even before the Caribs, the peaceful and kindly Arauacos were also exterminated. Simply speaking, the two groups suffered jointly one of the greatest ethnocides recorded in history. (Needless to say, this line of action is still more alive than the earlier one.) In relation to this fact, it will always be necessary to point out the case of those men who, being on the fringe both of utopianism (which has nothing to do with the actual America) and of the shameless ideology of plunder, stood in their midst opposed to the conduct of the colonialists and passionately, lucidly, and valiantly defended the flesh-and-blood aborigine. In the forefront of such men stands the magnificent figure of Father Bartolomé de las Casas, whom Bolívar called "the apostle of America" and whom Martí extolled unreservedly. Unfortunately, such men were exceptions.

One of the most widely disseminated European utopian works is Montaigne's essay "De los caníbales" [On Cannibals], which appeared in 1580. There we find a presentation of those creatures who "retain alive and vigorous their genuine, their most useful and natural, virtues and properties."[6]

Giovanni Floro's English translation of the *Essays* was published in 1603. Not only was Floro a personal friend of Shakespeare, but the copy of the translation that Shakespeare owned and annotated is still extant. This piece of information would be of no further importance but for the fact that it proves beyond a shadow of doubt that the *Essays* was one of the direct sources of Shakespeare's last great work, *The Tempest* (1612). Even one of the characters of the play, Gonzalo, who incarnates the Renaissance humanist, at one point closely glosses entire lines from Floro's Montaigne, originating precisely in the essay on cannibals. This fact makes the form in which Shakespeare presents his character *Caliban/cannibal* even stranger. Because if in Montaigne — in this case, as unquestionable literary source for Shakespeare — "there is nothing barbarous and savage in that nation . . . , except that each man calls barbarism whatever is not his own practice,"[7] in Shakespeare, on the other hand, *Caliban/cannibal* is a savage and deformed slave who cannot be degraded enough. What has happened is simply that in depicting Caliban, Shakespeare, an implacable realist, here takes *the other option* of the emerging bourgeois world. Regarding the utopian vision, it does indeed exist in the work but is unrelated to Caliban; as was said before, it is expressed by the harmonious humanist Gonzalo. Shakespeare thus confirms that both ways of considering the American, far from being in opposition, were perfectly reconcilable. As for the concrete man, present him in the guise of an animal, rob him of his land, enslave him so as to live from his toil, and at the right moment exterminate him; this latter, of course, only if there were someone who could be depended on to perform the arduous tasks in his stead. In one revealing passage, Prospero warns his daughter that they could not do without Caliban: "We cannot miss him: he does make our fire,/ Fetch in our wood, and serves in offices/ that profit us"(1.2.311–13). The utopian vision can and must do without men of flesh and blood. After all, *there is no such place.*

There is no doubt at this point that *The Tempest* alludes to America, that its island is the mythification of one of our islands. Astrana Marín, who mentions the "clearly Indian (American) ambience of the island," recalls some of the actual voyages along this continent that inspired Shakespeare and even furnished him, with slight variations, with the names of not a few of his characters: Miranda, Fernando, Sebastian, Alonso, Gonzalo, Setebos.[8] More important than this is the knowledge that Caliban is our Carib.

We are not interested in following all the possible readings that have been made of this notable work since its appearance,[9] and shall merely point out some interpretations. The first of these comes from Ernest Renan, who published his drama *Caliban: Suite de "La Tempête"* in 1878.[10] In this work, Caliban is the incarnation of the people presented in their worst light, except that this time his conspiracy against Prospero is successful and he achieves power—which ineptitude and corruption will surely prevent him from retaining. Prospero lurks in the darkness awaiting his revenge, and Ariel disappears. This reading owes less to Shakespeare than to the Paris Commune, which had taken place only seven years before. Naturally, Renan was among the writers of the French bourgeoisie who savagely took part against the prodigious "assault of heaven."[11] Beginning with this event, his antidemocratic feeling stiffened even further. "In his *Philosophical Dialogues*," Lidsky tells us, "he believes that the solution would lie in the creation of an *élite* of intelligent beings who alone would govern and posses the secrets of science."[12] Characteristically, Renan's aristocratic and prefascist elitism and his hatred of the common people of his country are united with an even greater hatred for the inhabitants of the colonies. It is instructive to hear him express himself along these lines.

> We aspire [he says] not only to equality but to domination. The country of a foreign race must again be a country of serfs, of agricultural laborers or industrial workers. It is not a question of eliminating the inequalities among men but of broadening them and making them law.[13]

And on another occasion:

> The regeneration of the inferior or bastard races by the superior races is within the providential human order. With us, the common man is nearly always a *declassé* nobleman, his heavy hand is better suited to handling the sword than the menial tool. Rather than work he chooses to fight, that is, he returns to his first state. *Regere imperio populos*—that is our vocation. Pour forth this all-consuming activity onto countries which, like China, are crying aloud for foreign conquest. . . . Nature has made a race of workers, the Chinese race, with its marvelous manual dexterity and almost no sense of honor; govern them with justice, levying from them, in return for the blessing of such a government, an ample allowance for the conquering race, and they will be satisfied; a race of tillers of the soil, the black . . . a race of masters and soldiers, the European race. . . . *Let each do that which he is made for, and all will be well.*[14]

It is unnecessary to gloss these lines, which, as Césaire rightly says, came from the pen not of Hitler but of the French humanist Ernest Renan.

The initial destiny of the Caliban myth on our own American soil is a surprising one. Twenty years after Renan had published his *Caliban*—in other words, in 1898—the United States intervened in the Cuban war of independence against Spain and subjected Cuba to its tutelage, converting her in 1902 into her first *neocolony* (and holding her until 1959), while Puerto Rico and the Philippines became colonies of a tradtional nature. The fact—which had been anticipated by Martí years before—moved the Latin-American *intelligentsia*. Elsewhere I have recalled that "ninety-eight" is not only a Spanish date that gives its name to a complex group of writers and thinkers of that country, but it is also, and perhaps most importantly, a Latin-American data that should serve to designate a no less complex group of writers and thinkers on this side of the Atlantic, generally known by the vague name of *modernistas*.[15] It is "ninety-eight"—the visible presence of North American imperialism in Latin America—already foretold by Martí, which informs the later work of someone like Darío or Rodó.

In a speech given by Paul Groussac in Buenos Aires on 2 May 1898, we have an early example of how Latin-American writers of the time would react to this situation:

> Since the Civil War and the brutal invasion of the West [he says], the
> *Yankee* spirit had rid itself completely of its formless and
> "Calibanesque" body, and the Old World has contemplated with
> disquiet and terror the newest civilization that intends to supplant our
> own, declared to be in decay.[16]

The Franco-Argentine writer Groussac feels that "our" civilization (obviously understanding by that term the civilization of the "Old World," of which we Latin Americans would, curiously enough, be a part) is menaced by the Calibanesque Yankee. It seems highly improbable that the Algerian or Vietnamese writer of the time, trampled underfoot by French colonialism, would have been ready to subscribe to the first part of such a criterion. It is also frankly strange to see the Caliban symbol—in which Renan could with exactitude see, if only to abuse, the people—being applied to the United States. But nevertheless, despite this blurred focus—characteristic, on the other hand, of Latin America's unique situation—Groussac's reaction implies a clear rejection of the Yankee danger by Latin-American writers. This is not, however, the first time that such a rejection was expressed on our continent. Apart from cases of Hispanic writers such as Bolívar and Martí, among others, Brazilian literature presents the example of Joaquín de Sousa Andrade, or Sousândrade, in whose strange poem, *O Guesa Errante*, stanza 10 is dedicated to "O inferno Wall Street," "a *Walpurgisnacht* of corrupt stockbrokers, petty politicians, and businessmen."[17] There is besides

José Verissimo, who in an 1890 treatise on national education impugned the United States with his "I admire them, but I don't esteem them."

We do not know whether the Uraguayan José Enrique Rodó—whose famous phrase on the United States, "I admire them, but I don't love them," coincides literally with Verissimo's observation—knew the work of that Brazilian thinker but it is certain that he was familiar with Groussac's speech, essential portions of which were reproduced in *La Razón* of Montevideo on 6 May 1898. Developing and embellishing the idea outlined in it, Rodó published in 1900, at the age of twenty-nine, one of the most famous works of Latin-American literature: *Ariel*. North American civilization is implicitly presented there as Caliban (scarcely mentioned in the work), while Ariel would come to incarnate—or should incarnate—the best of what Rodó did not hesitate to call more than once "our civilization" (223, 226). In his words, just as in those of Groussac, this civilization was identified not only with "our Latin America" (239) but with ancient Romania, if not with the Old World as a whole. The identification of Caliban with the United States, proposed by Groussac and popularized by Rodó, was certainly a mistake. Attacking this error from one angle, José Vasconcelos commented that "if the Yankees were only Caliban, they would not represent any great danger."[18] But this is doubtless of little importance next to the relevant fact that the danger in question had clearly been pointed out. As Benedetti rightly observed, "Perhaps Rodó erred in naming the danger, but he did not err in his recognition of where it lay."[19]

Sometime afterward, the French writer Jean Guéhenno—who, although surely aware of the work by the colonial Rodó, knew of course Renan's work from memory—restated the latter's Caliban thesis in his own *Caliban parle* [Caliban speaks], published in Paris in 1929. This time, however, the Renan identification of Caliban *with* the people is accompanied by a positive evaluation of Caliban. One must be grateful to Guéhenno's book—and it is about the only thing for which gratitude is due—for having offered for the first time an appealing version of the character.[20] But the theme would have required the hand or the rage of a Paul Nizan to be effectively realized.[21]

Much sharper are the observations of the Argentine Aníbal Ponce, in his 1935 work *Humanismo burgués y humanismo proletario*. The book—which a student of Che's thinking conjectures must have exercised influence on the latter[22]—devotes the third chapter to "Ariel; or, The Agony of an Obstinate Illusion." In commenting on *The Tempest*, Ponce says that "those four beings embody an entire era: Prospero is the enlightened despot who loves the Renaissance; Miranda, his progeny; Caliban, the suffering masses [Ponce will then quote Renan, but not Guéhenno]; and Ariel, the genius of the air without any ties to life."[23] Ponce points up the equivocal nature of Caliban's presentation, one that reveals "an enormous injustice on the part of a master." In Ariel he sees the intellectual, tied to Prospero in "less burdensome and crude a way than Caliban, but also in his service." His analysis of the conception of the intellectual ("mixture of slave and mercenary") coined by Renaissance humanism, a concept that "taught as nothing else could an indifference to action and an acceptance of the established order" and that even today is for the intellectual in the bourgeois world "the educational ideal of the governing classes," constitutes one of the most penetrating essays written on the theme in our America.

But this examination, although made by a Latin American, still took only the European world into account. For a new reading of *The Tempest*—for a new consideration of the problem—it was necessary to await the emergence of the colonial countries, which begins around the time of the Second World War. That abrupt presence led the busy technicians of the United Nations to invent, between 1944 and 1945, the term *economically underdeveloped area* in order to dress in attractive (and profoundly confusing) verbal garb what had until then been called *colonial area,* or *backward areas.*[24]

Concurrently with this emergence there appeared in Paris in 1950 O. Mannoni's book *Psychologie de la colonisation*. Significantly, the English edition of this book (New York, 1956) was to be called *Prospero and Caliban: The Psychology of Colonization*. To approach his subject, Mannoni has created, no less, what he calls the "Prospero complex," defined as "the sum of those unconscious neurotic tendencies that delineate at the same time the 'picture' of the paternalist colonial and the portrait of 'the racist whose daughter has been the object of an [imaginary] attempted rape at the hands of an inferior being.' "[25] In this book, probably for the first time, Caliban is identified with the colonial. But the odd theory that the latter suffers from a "Prospero complex" that leads him neurotically to require, even to anticipate, and naturally to accept the presence of Prospero/colonizer is roundly rejected by Frantz Fanon in the fourth chapter ("The So-Called Dependence Complex of Colonized Peoples") of his 1952 book *Black Skin, White Masks*.

Although he is (apparently) the first writer in our world to assume our identification with Caliban, the Barbadian writer George Lamming is unable to break the circle traced by Mannoni:

> Prospero [says Lamming] has given Caliban language; and with it an
> unstated history of consequences, an unknown history of future
> intentions. This gift of language meant not English, in particular, but
> speech and concept as a way, a method, a necessary avenue towards
> areas of the self which could not be reached in any other way. It is this
> way, entirely Prospero's enterprise, which makes Caliban aware of
> possibilities. Therefore, all of Caliban's future—for future is the very
> name of possibilities—must derive from Prospero's experiment, which is
> also his risk. Provided there is no extraordinary departure which
> explodes all of Prospero's premises, then Caliban and his future now
> belong to Prospero . . . Prospero lives in the absolute certainty that

Language, which is his gift to Caliban, is the very prison in which
Caliban's achievements will be realized and restricted.[26]

In the decade of the 1960s, the new reading of *The Tempest* ultimately established its hegemony. In *The Living World of Shakespeare* (1964), the Englishman
John Wain will tell us that Caliban

> has the pathos of the exploited peoples everywhere, poignantly
> expressed at the beginning of a three-hundred-year wave of European
> colonization; even the lowest savage wishes to be left alone rather than
> be "educated" and made to work for someone else, and there is an
> undeniable justice in his complaint: "For I am all the subjects that you
> have,/ Which once was mine own king." Prospero retorts with the
> inevitable answer of the colonist: Caliban has gained in knowledge and
> skill (though we recall that he already knew how to build dams to catch
> fish, and also to dig pig-nuts from the soil, as if this were the English
> countryside). Before being employed by Prospero, Caliban had no
> language: " . . . thou didst not, savage,/ Know thy own meaning, but
> wouldst gabble like/ A thing most brutish." However, this kindness has
> been rewarded with ingratitude. Caliban, allowed to live in Prospero's
> cell, has made an attempt to ravish Miranda. When sternly reminded of
> this, he impertinently says, with a kind of slavering guffaw, "Oh ho!
> Oh ho!—would it have been done!/ Thou didst prevent me; I had
> peopled else/ This isle with Calibans." Our own age [Wain concludes],
> which is much given to using the horrible word "miscegenation," ought
> to have no difficulty in understanding this passage.[27]

At the end of that same decade, in 1969, and in a highly significant manner,
Caliban would be taken up with pride as our symbol by three Antillian writers—
each of whom expresses himself in one of the three great colonial languages of
the Caribbean. In that year, independently of one another, the Martinican writer
Aimé Césaire published his dramatic work in French *Une tempête: Adaptation de
"La Tempête" de Shakespeare pour un théâtre nègre;* the Barbadian Edward
Brathwaite, his book of poems *Islands,* in English, among which there is one
dedicated to "Caliban" and the author of these lines, an essay in Spanish, "Cuba
hasta Fidel," which discusses our identification with Caliban.[28] In Césaire's
work the characters are the same as those of Shakespeare. Ariel, however, is a
mulatto slave, and Caliban is a black slave; in addition, Eshzú, "a black god-
devil" appears. Prospero's remark when Ariel returns, full of scruples, after having unleashed—following Prospero's orders but against his won conscience—the
tempest with which the work begins is curious indeed: "Come now!" Prospero
says to him, "Your crisis! It's always the same with intellectuals!" Brathwaite's
poem called "Caliban" is dedicated, signficantly, to Cuba: "In Havana that
morning . . . " writes Brathwaite, "It was December second, nineteen fifty-six./

It was the first of August eighteen thirty-eight./ It was the twelfth October four-
teen ninety-two./ How many bangs how many revolutions?"[29]

Our Symbol

Our symbol then is not Ariel, as Rodó thought, but rather Caliban. This is something that we, the *mestizo* inhabitants of these same isles where Caliban lived, see
with particular clarity: Prospero invaded the islands, killed our ancestors, enslaved Caliban, and taught him his language to make himself understood. What
else can Caliban do but use that same language—today he has no other—to curse
him, to wish that the "red plague" would fall on him? I know no other metaphor
more expressive of our cultural situation, of our reality. From Túpac Amaru, *Ti-
radentes,* Toussaint-Louverture, Simón Bolívar, Father Hidalgo, José Artigas,
Bernardo O'Higgins, Benito Juárez, Antonio Maceo, and José Martí, to Emi-
liano Zapata, Augusto César Sandino, Julio Antonio Mella, Pedro Albizu
Campos, Lázaro Cárdenas, Fidel Castro, and Ernesto Che Guevara, from the
Inca Garcilaso de la Vega, the *Aleijadinho,* the popular music of the Antilles,
José Hernández, Eugenio María de Hostos, Manuel González Prada, Rubén
Darío (yes, when all is said and done), Baldomero Lillo, and Horacio Quiroga, to
Mexican muralism, Heitor Villa-Lobos, César Vallejo, José Carlos Mariátegui,
Ezequiel Martínez Estrada, Carlos Gardel, Pablo Neruda, Alejo Carpentier, Ni-
colás Guillén, Aimé Césaire, José María Arguedas, Violeta Parra, and Frantz Fa-
non—what is our history, what is our culture, if not the history and culture of
Caliban?

As regards Rodó, if it is indeed true that he erred in his symbols, as has already been said, it is no less true that he was able to point with clarity to the
greatest enemy of our culture in his time—and in ours—and that is enormously
important. Rodó's limitations (and this is not the moment to elucidate them) are
responsible for what he saw unclearly or failed to see at all.[30] But what is worthy
of note in his case is what he did indeed see and what continued to retain a certain
amount of validity and even virulence.

> Despite his failings, omissions, and ingenuousness [Benedetti has also
> said], Rodó's vision of the Yankee phenomenon, rigorously situated in
> its historical context, was in its time the first launching pad for other
> less ingenuous, better informed and more foresighted formulations to
> come. . . . the almost prophetic substance of Rodó's Arielism still
> retains today a certain amount of validity.[31]

These observations are supported by indisputable realities. We Cubans become well aware that Rodó's vision fostered later, less ingenuous, and more radical formulations when we simply consider the work of our own Julio Antonio
Mella, on whose development the influence of Rodó was decisive. In "Intelec-

tuales y tartufos" [Intellectuals and Tartuffes] (1924), a vehement work written at the age of twenty-one, Mella violently attacks the false intellectual values of the time—opposing them with such names as Unamuno, José Vasconcelos, Ingenieros, and Varona. He writes, "The intellectual is the worker of the mind. The worker! That is, the only man who in Rodó's judgment is worthy of life, . . . he who takes up his pen against iniquity just as others take up the plow to fecundate the earth, or the sword to liberate peoples, or a dagger to execute tyrants."[32]

Mella would again quote Rodó with devotion during that year[33] and in the following year he was to help found the Ariel Polytechnic Institute in Havana.[34] It is opportune to recall that in this same year, 1925, Mella was also among the founders of Cuba's first Communist party. Without a doubt, Rodó's *Ariel* served as a "launching pad" for the meteoric revolutionary career of this first organic Marxist-Leninist in Cuba (who was also one of the first on the continent.)

As further examples of the relative validity that Rodó's anti-Yankee argument retains even in our own day, we can point to enemy attempts to disarm such an argument. A strange case is that of Emir Rodríguez Monegal, for whom *Ariel,* in addition to "material for philosophic or sociological meditation, *also* contains pages of a polemic nature on political problems *of the moment.* And it was precisely this *secondary* but undeniable condition that determined its immediate popularity and dissemination." Rodó's essential position against North American penetration would thus appear to be an afterthought, a *secondary* fact in the work. It is known, however, that Rodó conceived it immediately after American intervention in Cuba in 1898, *as a response to the deed.* Rodríguez Monegal says:

> The work thus projected was *Ariel.* In the final version *only two direct allusions* are found to the historical fact that was its primary motive force; . . . both allusions enable us to appreciate how Rodó has *transcended* the initial historical circumstance to arrive fully at the essential problem: the proclaimed decadence of the Latin race.[35]

The fact that a servant of imperialism such as Rodríguez Monegal, afflicted with the same "Nordo-mania" that Rodó denounced in 1900, tries so coarsely to emasculate Rodó's work, only proves that it does indeed retain a certain virulence in its formulation—something that we would approach today from other perspectives and with other means. An analysis of *Ariel*—and this is absolutely not the occasion to make one—would lead us also to stress how, despite his background and his antiJacobianism, Rodó combats in it the antidemocratic spirit of Renan and Nietzsche (in whom he finds "an abominable, reactionary spirit" [224]) and exalts democracy, moral values, and emulation. But undoubtedly the rest of the work has lost the immediacy that its gallant confrontation of the United States and the defense of our values still retains.

Put into perspective, it is almost certain that these lines would not bear the name they have were it not for Rodó's book, and I prefer to consider them also as a homage to the great Uruguayan, whose centenary is being celebrated this year. That the homage contradicts him on not a few points is not strange. Medardo Vitier has already observed that "if there should be a return to Rodó, I do not believe that it would be to adopt the solution he offered concerning the interests of the life of the spirit, but rather to reconsider the problem."[36]

In proposing Caliban as our symbol, I am aware that it is not entirely ours, that it is also an alien elaboration, although in this case based on our concrete realities. But how can this alien quality be entirely avoided? The most venerated word in Cuba—*mambí*—was disparagingly imposed on us by our enemies at the time of the war for independence, and we still have not totally deciphered its meaning. It seems to have an African root, and in the mouth of the Spanish colonists implied the idea that all *independentistas* were so many black slaves—emancipated by that very war for independence—who of course constituted the bulk of the liberation army. The *independentistas,* white and black, adopted with honor something that colonialism meant as an insult. This is the dialectic of Caliban. To offend us they call us *mambí,* they call us *black;* but we reclaim as a mark of glory the honor of considering ourselves descendants of the *mambí,* descendants of the rebel, runaway, *independentista* black—*never* descendants of the slave holder. Nevertheless, Propero, as we well know, taught his language to Caliban and, consequently, gave him a name. But is this his true name? Let us listen to this speech made in 1971:

> To be completely precise, we still do not even have a name; we still
> have no name; we are practically unbaptized—whether as Latin
> Americans, Ibero-Americans, Indo-Americans. For the imperialists, we
> are nothing more than despised and despicable peoples. At least that
> was what we were. Since Girón they have begun to change their
> thinking. Racial contempt—to be a Creole, to be a mestizo, to be black,
> to be simply, a Latin American, is for them contemptible.[37]

This, naturally, is Fidel Castro on the tenth anniversary of the victory at Playa Girón.

To assume our condition as Caliban implies rethinking our history from the *other* side, from the viewpoint of the *other* protagonist. The *other* protagonist of *The Tempest* (or, as we might have said ourselves, *The Hurricane*) is not of course Ariel but, rather, Prospero.[38] There is no real Ariel-Caliban polarity: both are slaves in the hands of Prospero, the foreign magician. But Caliban is the rude and unconquerable master of the island, while Ariel, a creature of the air, although also a child of the isle, is the intellectual—as both Ponce and Césire have seen.

Again Martí

This conception of our culture had already been articulately expressed and defended in the last century by the first among us to understand clearly the concrete situation of what he called—using a term I have referred to several times—"our mestizo America": José Martí[39] to whom Rodó planned to dedicate the first Cuban edition of *Ariel* and about whom he intended to write a study similar to those he devoted to Bolívar and Artigas (see 1359, 1375), a study that in the end he unfortunately never realized.

Although he devoted numerous pages to the topic, the occasion on which Martí offered his ideas on this point in a most organic and concise manner was in his 1891 article "Our America." I will limit myself to certain essential quotations. But I should first like to offer some observations on the destiny of Martí's work.

During Martí's lifetime, the bulk of his work, scattered throughout a score of continental newspapers, enjoyed widespread fame. We know that Rubén Darío called Martí "Maestro" (as, for other reasons, his political followers would also call him during his lifetime) and considered him the Latin American whom he most admired. We shall soon see, on the other hand, how the harsh judgments on the United States that Martí commonly made in his articles, equally well know in his time, were the cause of acerbic criticism by the proYankee Sarmiento. But the particular manner in which Martí's writings circulated—he made use of journalism, oratory, and letter but *never published a single book*—bears no little responsibility for the relative oblivion into which the work of the Cuban hero fell after his death in 1895. This alone explains the fact that nine years after his death—and twelve from the time Martí stopped writing for the continental press, devoted as he was after 1892 to his political tasks—an author as absolutely ours and as far above suspicion as the twenty-year-old Pedro Henríquez Ureña could write in 1904, in an article on Rodó's *Ariel,* that the latter's opinions on the United States are "much more severe than those formulated by two of the greatest thinkers and most brilliant psycho-sociologists of the Antilles: Hostos and Martí."[40] Insofar as this refers to Martí, the observation is completely erroneous; and given the exemplary honesty of Henríquez Ureña, it led me, first, to suspect and later, to verify that it was due simply to the fact that during this period the great Dominican had not read, *had been unable to read,* Martí adequately. Martí was hardly *published* at the time. A text such as the fundamental "Our America" is a good example of this fate. Readers of the Mexican newspaper *El Partido Liberal* could have read it on 30 January 1891. It is possible that some other local newspaper republished it,[41] although the most recent edition of Martí's *Complete Works* does not indicate anything in this regard. But it is most likely that those who did not have the good fortune to obtain that newspaper knew nothing about the article—the most important document published in America from the end of the past century until the appearance in 1962 of the Second Declaration of Havana—for almost twenty years, at the end of which time it appeared in book form (Havana, 1910) in the irregular collection in which publication of the complete works of Martí was begun. For this reason Manuel Pedro González is correct when he asserts that during the first quarter of this century the new generations did not know Martí. "A minimal portion of his work" was again put into circulation, starting with the eight volumes published by Alberto Ghiraldo in Madrid in 1925. Thanks to the most recent appearance of several editions of his complete works—actually still incomplete—"he has been rediscovered and reevaluated."[42] González is thinking above all of the dazzling literary qualities of this work ("the literary glory" as he says). Could we not add something, then, regarding the works' fundamental ideological aspects? Without forgetting very important prior contributions, there are sill some essential points that explain why today, after the triumph of the Cuban Revolution and because of it, Martí is being "rediscovered and reevaluated." It was no mere coincidence that in 1953 Fidel named Martí as the intellectual author of the attack on the Moncade Barracks nor that Che should use a quotation from Martí—"it is the hour of the furnace, and only light should be seen"—to open his extremely important "Message to the Tricontinental Congress" in 1967. If Benedetti could say that Rodó's time "was different from our own . . . his true place, his true temporal homeland was the nineteenth century," we must say, on the other hand, that Martí's true place was the future and, for the moment, this era of ours, which simply cannot be understood without a thorough knowledge of this work.

Now, if that knowledge, because of the curious circumstances alluded to, was denied or available only in a limited way to the early generations of this century, who frequently had to base their defense of subsequent radical arguments on a "first launching pad" as well-intentioned but at the same time as weak as the nineteenth-century work *Ariel,* what can we say of more recent authors to whom editions of Martí are now available but who nevertheless persist in ignoring him? I am thinking, of course, not of scholars more or less ignorant of our problems but, on the contrary, of those who maintain a consistently anticolonialist attitude. The only explanation of this situation is a painful one: we have been so thoroughly steeped in colonialism that we read with real respect only those anticolonialist authors *disseminated from the metropolis.* In this way we cast aside the greatest lesson of Martí; thus, we are barely familiar with Artigas, Recabarren, Mella, and even Mariátegui and Ponce. And I have the sad suspicion that if the extraordinary texts of Che Guevara have enjoyed the greatest dissemination ever accorded a Latin American, the fact that he is read with such avidity by our people is to a certain extent due to the prestige his name has even in the metropolitan capitals—where, to be sure, he is frequently the object of the most shameless manipulation. For consistency in our anticolonialist attitude we must in effect turn to those of our people who have incarnated and illustrated that attitude in their behavior and thinking.[43] And for this, there is no case more useful than that of Martí.

I know of no other Latin-American author who has given so immediate and so coherent an answer to another question put to me by my interlocutor, the European journalist whom I mentioned at the beginning of these lines (and whom, if he did not exist, I would have had to invent, although this would have deprived me of his friendship, which I trust will survive this monologue): "What relationship," this guileless wit asked me, "does Borges have to the Incas?" Borges is almost a reductio ad absurdum and, in any event, I shall discuss him later. But it is only right and fair to ask what relationship we, the present inhabitants of this America in whose zoological and cultural heritage Europe has played an unquestionable part, have to the primitive inhabitants of this same America—those peoples who constructed or were in the process of constructing admirable cultures and who were exterminated or martyred by Europeans of various nations, about whom neither a white nor black legend can be build, only an infernal truth of blood, that, together with such deeds as the enslavement of Africans, constitutes their eternal dishonor. Martí, whose father was from Valencia and whose mother was from the Canaries, who wrote the most prodigious Spanish of his—and our—age, and who came to have the greatest knowledge of the Euro–North American culture ever possessed by a man of our American, also asked this question. He answered it as follows: "We are descended from Valencian fathers and Canary Island mothers and feel the inflamed blood of Tamanaco and Paramaconi coursing through our veins; we see the blood that fell amid the brambles of Mount Calvary as our own, along with that shed by the naked and heroic Caracas as they struggled breast to breast with the gonzalos in their iron-plated armor."[44]

I presume that the reader, if he or she is not a Venezuelan, will be unfamiliar with the names evoked by Martí. So was I. This lack of familiarity is but another proof of our subjection to the colonialist perspective of history that has been imposed on us, causing names, dates, circumstances, and truths to vanish from our consciousness. Under other circumstances—but closely related to these—did not the bourgeois version of history try to erase the heroes of the Commune of 1871, the martyrs of 1 May 1886 (significantly reclaimed by Martí)? At any rate, Tamanaco, Paramaconi, "the naked and heroic Caracas" were natives of what is today called Venezuela, of *Carib blood, the blood of Caliban,* coursing through his veins. This will not be the only time he expresses such an idea, which is central to his thinking.[45] Again making use of such heroes, he was to repeat sometime later: "We must stand with Guaicaipuro, Paramaconi [heroes of Venezuela, probably of Carib origin], and not with the flames that burned them, nor with the ropes that bound them, nor with the steel that beheaded them, nor with the dogs that devoured them."[46] Martí's rejection of the ethnocide that Europe practiced is *total.* No less total is his identification with the American peoples that offered heroic resistance to the invader, and in whom Martí say the natural forerunners of

the Latin-American *independentistas*. This explains why in the notebook in
which this last quotation appears, he continues writing, almost without transition, on Aztec mythology ("no less beautiful than the Greek"), on the ashes of
Quetzacoatl, on "Ayachucho on the solitary plateau," on "Bolívar, like the
rivers."[47]

Martí, however, dreams not of a restoration now impossible but of the future
integration of our America—an America rising organically from a firm grasp of
its true roots to the heights of authentic modernity. For this reason, the first quotation in which he speaks of feeling valiant Carib blood coursing through his
veins continues as follows:

> It is good to open canals, to promote schools, to create steamship lines,
> to keep abreast of one's own time, to be on the side of the vanguard in
> the beautiful march of humanity. But in order not to falter because of a
> lack of spirit or the vanity of a false spirit, it is good also to nourish
> oneself through memory and admiration, through righteous study and
> loving compassion, on that fervent spirit of the natural surroundings in
> which one is born—a spirit matured and quickened by those of every
> race that issues from such surroundings and finds its final repose in
> them. Politics and literature flourish only when they are direct. The
> American intelligence is an indigenous plumage. Is it not evident that
> America itself was paralyzed by the same blow that paralyzed the
> Indian? And until the Indian is caused to walk, America itself will not
> begin to walk well. ["AAA," 337]

Martí's identification with our aboriginal culture was thus accompanied by a
complete sense of the concrete tasks imposed upon him by his circumstances. Far
from hampering him, that identification nurtured in him the most radical and
modern criteria of his time in the colonial countries.

Naturally, Martí's approach to the Indian was also applied to the black.[48] Unfortunately, while in his day serious inquiries into American aboriginal cultures
(which Martí studied passionately) had already been undertaken, only in the
twentieth century would then appear similar studies of African cultures and their
considerable contribution to the makeup of our mestizo America (see Frobenius,
Delafosse, Suret-Canale; Ortiz, Ramos, Herskovits, Roumain, Metraux,
Bastide, Franco).[49] And Martí died five years before the dawning of our century.
In any event, in his treatment of Indian culture and in his concrete behavior toward the black, he left a very clear outline of a "battle plan" in this area.

This is the way in which Martí forms his Calibanesque vision of the culture of
what he called "our America." Martí is, as Fidel was later to be, aware of how
difficult it is even to find a name that in designating us defines us conceptually.
For this reason, after several attempts, he favored that modest descriptive formula that above and beyond race, language, and secondary circumstances em-

braces the communities that live, with their common problems, "from the [Rio] Bravo to Patagonia," and that are distinct from "European America." I have already said that although it is found scattered throughout his very numerous writings, this conception of our culture is aptly summarized in the article-manifesto "Our America," and I direct the reader to it: to his insistence upon the idea that one cannot "rule new peoples with a singular and violent composition, with laws inherited from four centuries of free practice in the United States, or nineteen centuries of monarchy in France. One does not stop the blow in the chest of the plainsman's horse with one of Hamilton's decrees. One does not clear the congealed blood of the Indian race with a sentence of Sieyès"; to his deeply rooted concept that "the imported book has been conquered in America by the natural man. Natural men have conquered the artificial men of learning. *The authentic mestizo has conquered the exotic Creole"* (my emphasis); and finally to his fundamental advice:

> The European university must yield to the American university. The history of America, from the Incas to the present, must be taught letter perfect, even if that of the Argonauts of Greece is not taught. Our own Greece is preferable to that Greece that is not ours. We have greater need of it. National politicians must replace foreign and exotic politicians. Graft the world onto our republics, but the trunk must be that of our republics. And let the conquered pedant be silent: there is no homeland of which the individual can be more proud than our unhappy American republics.

The Real Life of a False Dilemma

It is impossible not to see in this text—which, as has been said, summarizes in lightning fashion Martí's judgment on this essential problem—his violent rejection of the imposition of Prospero ("the European university [,] . . . the European book [,] . . . the Yankee book"), which *"must yield"* to the reality of Caliban ("the [Latin] American university [,] . . . the Latin American enigma"): "The history of America, from the Incas to the present, must be taught letter perfect even, if that of the Argonauts of Greece is not taught. Our own Greece is preferable to that Greece that is not ours." And later: "Common cause must be made with the oppressed so as to secure the system against the interest and customs of the oppressors."

But our America has also heard, expressed with vehemence by a talented and energetic man who died three years before Martí's work appeared, the thesis that was the exact opposite: the thesis of Prospero.[50] The interlocutors were not called then Prospero and Caliban, but rather *Civilization and Barbarism,* the title that the Argentinean Domingo Faustino Sarmiento gave to the first edition (1845) of his great book on Facundo Quiroga. I do not believe that autobiographical con-

fessions are of much interest here, but since I have already mentioned, by way of
self-inflicted punishment, the forgettable pleasures of the westerns and Tarzan
films by which we were innoculated, unbeknownst to us, with the ideology that
we verbally repudiated in the Nazis (I was twelve years old when the Second
World War was at its height), I must also confess that only a few years afterward,
I read this book passionately. In the margins of my old copy, I find my enthu-
siasms, my rejections of the "tyrant of the Republic of Argentina" who had exclaimed, "Traitors to the American cause!" I also find, a few pages later, the
comment, "It is strange how one thinks of Perón." It was many years later, specifically after the triumph of the Cuban Revolution in 1959 (when we began to
live and to read the world in another way), that I understood I had not been on the
best side in that otherwise remarkable book. It was not possible to be simultaneously in agreement with *Facundo* and with "Our America." What is more,
"Our America" — along with a large part of Martí's entire work — is an implicit,
and at times explicit, dialogue with the Sarmiento theses. If not, what then does
this lapidary sentence of Martí's mean: "*There is no battle between civilization
and barbarism,* only between false erudition and nature." Eight years before
"Our America" appeared (1891) — within Sarmiento's lifetime — Martí had already spoken (in the sentence I have quoted more than once) of the "pretext that
civilization, which is the vulgar name under which contemporary European man
operates, has the natural right to seize the land of foreigners, which is the name
given by those who desire foreign lands to every contemporary human being who
does not come from Europe or European America."[51] In both cases, Martí *rejects* the *false* dichotomy that Sarmiento, falling into the trap adroitly set by the
colonizer, takes for granted. For this reason, when I said sometime ago that "in
coming out on the side of 'barbarism' Martí foreshadows Fanon and our
Revolution"[52] (a phrase that some hasty people, without noticing the quotation
marks, misunderstood — as if Fanon, Fidel, and Che were apostles of barbarism),
I wrote "barbarism" in this way, between quotation marks, to indicate that in
fact there was not such state. The presumed barbarism of our peoples was invented with crude cynicism by "those who desire foreign lands"; those who,
with equal effrontery, give the "popular name" of "civilization" to the "contemporary" human being who comes "from Europe or European America."
What was surely more painful for Martí was to see a man of our America — a man
whom, despite incurable differences, he admired in his positive aspects[53] — fall
into this very grave error. Thinking of figures such as Sarmiento, it was Martínez
Estrada (who had *previously* written so many pages extolling Sarmiento) who in
1962 wrote in his book *Diferencias y semejanzas entre los países de la América
Latina* [Similarities and Differences among Latin-American Countries]:

> We can immediately establish the premise that those who have worked,
> in some cases patriotically, to shape social life in complete accordance

with models of other highly developed countries, whose practices are the result of an organic process over the course of centuries, have betrayed the cause of the true emancipation of Latin America.[54]

I lack the necessary information to discuss here the virtues and defects of this bourgeois antagonist and shall limit myself to pointing out this opposition to Martí, and the coherence between his thought and conduct. As a postulator of *Civilization,* which he found incarnated in archetypal form in the United States, he advocated the extermination of the indigenous peoples according to the savage Yankee model; what is more, he adored that growing republic to the north that had by mid-century still not demonstrated so clearly the flaws that Martí would later discover. In both extremes — and they are precisely that: extremes, margins of their respective thinking — he and Martí differed irreconcilably.

Jaime Alazraki has studied with some care "El indigenismo de Martí y el antindigenismo de Sarmiento" [The indigenism of Martí and the anti-indigenism of Sarmiento].[55] I refer the reader interested in the subject to this essay; here I shall only draw on some of the quotations from the works of both included in that study. I have already mentioned some of Martí's observations on the Indian. Alazraki recalls others:

No more than peoples in blossom, no more than the bulbs of peoples, were those the valiant conquistador marched upon; with his subtle craftiness of the old-time opportunist, he discharged his powerful firearms. It was a historic misfortune and a natural crime. The well-formed stalk should have been left standing, the entire flowering work of Nature could then be seen in all its beauty. The conquistadors stole a page from the Universe!

And further:

Of all that greatness there remains in the museum scarcely a few gold cups, a few stones of polished obsidian shaped like a yoke, and one or two wrought rings. Tenochtitlán does not exist, nor Tulan, the city of the great fair, Texcuco, the city of the palaces, is no more. Indians of today, passing before the ruins, lower their heads and move their lips as if saying something; they do not put on their hats again until the ruins are left behind.

For Sarmiento, the history of America is the "bands of abject races, a great continent abandoned to savages incapable of progress." If we want to know how he interpreted the maxim of his compatriot Alberdi that "to govern is to populate," we must read this: "Many difficulties will be presented by the occupation of so extensive a country; but there will be no advantage comparable to that gained by the extinction of the savage tribes." That is to say, for Sarmiento, to govern is also to *depopulate* the nation of its Indians (and gauchos). And what of the heroes of the resistance against the Spaniards, those magnificent men whose rebellious blood Martí felt coursing through his veins? Sarmiento has also questioned himself about them. This is his response:

> For us, Colocolo, Lautaro, and Caupolicán, notwithstanding the noble
> and civilized garb with which they are adorned by Ercilla, are nothing
> more than a handful of loathesome Indians. We would have them
> hanged today were they to reappear in a war of the Araucanos against
> Chile, a country that has nothing to do with such rabble.

This naturally implies a vision of the Spanish conquest radically different from that upheld by Martí. For Sarmiento, "Spanish—repeated a hundred times in the odious sense of impious, immoral, ravisher and impostor—is synonymous with civilization, with the European tradition brought by them to these countries." And while for Martí, "there is no racial hatred, because there are no races," the author of *Conflicto y armonias de las razas en América* [Conflict and Harmony among the Races in America] bases himself thus on pseudoscientific theories:

> It may be very unjust to exterminate savages, suffocate rising
> civilizations, conquer peoples who are in possession of a privileged
> piece of land. But thanks to this injustice, America, instead of
> remaining abandoned to the savages, incapable of progress, is today
> occupied by the Caucasian race—the most perfect, the most intelligent,
> the most beautiful and most progressive of those that people the earth.
> Thanks to these injustices, Oceania is filled with civilized peoples, Asia
> begins to move under the European impulse, Africa sees the times of
> Carthage and the glorious days of Egypt reborn on her coats. Thus, the
> population of the world is subject to revolutions that recognize
> immutable laws; the strong races exterminate the weak ones and the
> civilized peoples supplant the savages in the possession of the earth.

There was no need then to cross the Atlantic and seek out Renan to hear such words: a man of this America was saying them. The fact is that if he did not learn them on this side of the ocean, they were at least reinforced for him here—not in our America but in the other, "European [,] America," of which Sarmiento was the most fanatical devotee in our mestizo lands during the nineteenth century. Although in that century there is no shortage of Latin Americans who adored the Yankees, our discovery of people among us equal to Sarmiento in their devotion to the United States would be due above all to the ranting seqoyism in which our twentieth-century Latin America has been so prodigal. What Sarmiento wanted for Argentina was exactly what the United States had achieved for itself. The last words he wrote (1888) were: "We shall catch up to the United States. . . . Let us become the United States." His travels in that country produced in him a genuine bedazzlement, a never-ending historical orgasm. He tried to establish in his homeland the bases for an enterprising bourgeoisie, similar to what he saw there. Its present fate makes any commentary unnecessary.

What Martí saw in the United States is also sufficiently well known that we need not dwell upon the point. Suffice it to recall that he was the first militant anti-imperialist of our continent; that he denounced over a period of fifteen years "the crude, inequitable, the decadent character of the United States, and the continued existence therein of all the violence, discord, immorality, and disorder for which the Hispano-American peoples are censured"[56]; that a few hours before his death on the battlefield, he confided in a letter to his great friend, the Mexican Manuel Mercado, "Everything I have done to this day, and everything I shall do is to that end [,] . . . to prevent in time the expansion of the United States into the Antilles and to prevent her from falling, with ever greater force, upon our American lands."[57]

Sarmiento did not remain silent before the criticism that Martí—frequently from the very pages of *La Nación*—leveled against his idolized United States. He commented on one occasion on this incredible boldness:

> Don José Martí lacks only one requirement to be a journalist . . . He has failed to regenerate himself, to educate himself, so to speak, to receive inspiration from the country in which he lives, as one receives food so as to convert it into life-giving blood. . . . I should like Martí to give us less of Martí, less of the purebred Spaniard, and less of the South American, and in exchange, a little more of the Yankee—the new type of modern man. . . . It is amusing to hear a Frenchman of the *Courier des États-Unis* laughing at the stupidities and political incompetence of the Yankees, whose institutions Gladstone proclaims the supreme work of the human race. But to criticize with magisterial airs that which a Latin American, a Spaniard, sees there, with a confetti of political judgement transmitted to him by the books of other nations—as if trying to see sunspots through a blurred glass—is to do the reader a very grave injustice and lead him down the path of perdition. . . . Let them not come to us, then, with their insolent humility of South Americans, semi-Indians and semi-Spaniards, to find evil.[58]

Sarmiento, who was as vehement in his praise as his invective, here places Martí among the "semi-Indians." This was in essence true and for Martí a point of pride; but we have already seen what it implied in the mouth of Sarmiento . . .

For these reasons, and despite the fact that highly esteemed writers have tried to point out possible similarities, I think it will be understood how difficult it is to accept a parallel between these two men, such as the one elaborated by Emeterio S. Santovenia in the 262 sloppy pages of *Genio y acción: Sarmiento y Martí*. A sample will suffice: according to this author, "Above and beyond the discrepancies in the achievements and limitations of their respective projections concerning America, there does emerge a coincidence [*sic*] in their evaluations [those of Sarmiento and Martí] of the Anglo-Saxon role in the development of political and social ideas that fertilized the tree of total emancipation in the New World."[59]

This luxuriant undergrowth of thought, syntax, and metaphor gives some indication of what our culture was like when we were part of the "free world," of which Mr. Santovenia (as well as being one of Batista's ministers in his moments of leisure) was so eminent a representative.

On the Free World

But the portion of the free world that corresponds to Latin America can boast today of much more memorable figures. There is Jorge Luis Borges, for example, whose name seems to be associated with "memorable." The Borges I have in mind is the one who only a short time ago dedicated his (presumably good) translation of Whitman's *Leaves of Grass* to United States President Richard Nixon. It is true that Borges wrote in 1926, "I want to speak to the Creoles—to those who feel their existence deeply rooted in our lands, not to those who think the sun and the moon are in Europe. This is a land of born exiles, of men nostalgic for the far-off and the foreign: they are the real gringos, regardless of their parentage, and I do not address myself to them." It is also true that Sarmiento is presented at that time as a "North American Indian brave, who loathed and misprized anything Creole."[60] But the fact is that *Borges* is not the one who has gone down in history. This "memorious" individual decided to forget the little book of his youth, that he wrote only a few years after having been a member of "the sect, the blunder, called Ultraism." In his eyes that book and the ideas in it were also a blunder. Pathetically faithful to his class,[61] it was a different Borges who would become so well known, attain such great circulation abroad, and experience the public acclaim of innumerable literary prizes—some of which are so obscure that he would seem to have awarded them himself. The Borges in question, to whom we shall dedicate a few lines here, is the one who echoes Sarmiento's grotesque "We belong to the Roman Empire," with this declaration not of 1926 but of 1955: "I believe that our tradition is Europe."[62]

It might seem strange that the ideological filiation of such an energetic and blustering pioneer would come to be manifest today in a man so sedate, a writer such as Borges—the archetypal representative of a bookish culture that on the surface seems far removed from Sarmiento's constant vitality. But this strangeness only demonstrates how accustomed we are to judging the superstructural products of our continent, if not of the whole world, without regard to their concrete structural realities. Except by considering these realities, how would we recognize the insipid disasters who are the bourgeois intellectuals of our time as descending from those vigorous and daring thinkers of the rising bourgeoisie? We need only consider our writers and thinkers in relation to the classes whose world view they expound in order to orient ourselves properly and outline their true filiations. The dialogue we have just witnessed between Sarmiento and Martí was, more than anything else, a class confrontation.

Independently of his (class) origin, Sarmiento is the implacable ideologue of an Argentine bourgeoisie that is attempting to transport bourgeois policies of the metropolitan centers (particularly those of North America) to its own country. To be successful, it must impose itself, like all bourgeoisies, upon the popular classes; it must exploit them physically and condemn them spiritually. The manner in which a bourgeoisie develops at the expense of the popular classes' brutalization is memorably demonstrated, taking England as an example, in some of the most impressive pages of *Das Kapital*. "European America," whose capitalism succeeded in expanding fabulously—unhampered as it was by the feudalistic order—added new circles of hell to England's achievements: the enslavement of the Negro and the extermination of the indomitable Indian. These were the models to which Sarmiento looked and which he proposed to follow faithfully. He is perhaps the most consequential and the most active of the bourgeois ideologues on our continent during the nineteenth century.

Martí, on the other hand, is a conscious spokesman of the exploited classes. "Common cause must be made with the oppressed," he told us, "so as to secure the system against the interests and customs of the oppressors." And, since beginning with the conquest Indians and blacks have been relegated to the base of the social pyramid, making common cause with the oppressed came largely to be the same as making common cause with Indians and blacks—which is what Martí does. These Indians and those blacks had been intermingling among themselves and with some whites, giving rise to the *mestizaje* that is at the root of our America, where—according to Martí—"the authentic mestizo has conquered the exotic Creole." Sarmiento is a ferocious racist because he is an ideologue of the exploiting classes, in whose ranks the "exotic Creole" is found, Martí is radically antiracist because he is a spokesman for the exploited classes, within which the three races are fusing. Sarmiento opposes what is essentially American in order to inculcate—with blood and fire, just as the conquistadors had tried to do—alien formulas here. Martí defends the autochthonous, the genuinely American. This does not mean, of course, that he foolishly rejected whatever positive elements might be offered by other realities: "Graft the world onto our republics," he said, "but the trunk must be that of our republics." Sarmiento also sought to graft the world onto our republics, but he would have their trunks uprooted in the process. For that reason, if the continuators of Martí are found in Mella and Vallejo, Fidel and Che, and in the new culture of revolutionary Latin America, the heirs of Sarmiento (in spite of his complexity) are, in the final analysis, the represenatives of the Argentine vice-bourgeoisie. They are, moreover, a defeated class, because the dream of bourgeois development that Sarmiento envisaged was not even a possibility. There was simply no way an eventual Argentine bourgeoisie could develop. Latin America was a late arrival to that fiesta, for as Mariátegui wrote: "The time of free competition in the capitalist economy has come to an end, in all areas and in every aspect. We are now in an era of monopolies, of empires. The Latin-American countries are experiencing a belated entry into competitive capitalism. The dominant positions are already well established. The fate of such countries, within the capitalist order, is that of simple colonies."[63]

Incorporated into what is called with a bit of unintentional humor the "free world," our countries—in spite of our shields, anthems, flags, and presidents—would inaugurate a new form of not being independent: neocolonialism. The bourgeoisie, for whom Sarmiento had outlined such delightful possibilities, became no more than an vice-bourgeoisie, a modest local shareholder in imperial exploitation—first the English, then the North American.

It is in this light that one sees more clearly the connections between Sarmiento—whose name is associated with grand pedagogical projects, immense spaces, railways, ships—and Borges, the mention of whom evokes mirrors that multiply the same miserable image, unfathomable labyrinths, and a sad, dimly lit library. But apart from this, if the "American-ness" of Sarmiento is always taken for granted (although it is obvious in him, this is not to say he represents the positive pole of that "American-ness"), I have never been able to understand why it is denied to Borges. Borges is a typical colonial writer, the representative among us of a now-powerless class for whom the act of writing—and he is well aware of this, for he is a man of diaboloical intelligence—is more like the act of reading. He is not a European writer; there is no European writer like Borges. But there are *many* European writers—from Iceland to the German expressionists—whom Borges has *read,* shuffled together, collated. European writers belong to very concrete and provincial traditions—reaching the extreme case of a Péguy, for example, who boasted of never having read anything but French authors. Apart from a few professors of philology, who recieve a salary for it, there is only one type of person who really knows in its entirety the literature of Europe: the colonial. Only in the case of mental imbalance can a learned Argentine writer ever boast of having read nothing but Argentine—or even Spanish-language—authors. And Borges is not imbalanced. On the contrary, he is an extremely lucid man, one who exemplifies Martí's idea that intelligence is only one—and not necessarily the best—part of a man.

The writing of Borges comes directly from his reading, in a peculiar process of phagocytosis that identifies him clearly as a colonial and the representative of a dying class. For him the creation par excellence of culture is a library; or better yet, a museum—a place where the products of culture from abroad are assem-

bled. A museum of horrors, of monsters, of splendors, of folkloric data and ar-
tifacts (those of Argentina seen with the eye of a curator)—the work of Borges,
written in a Spanish difficult to read without admiration, is one of the American
scandals of our time.

Unlike some other important Latin-American writers, Borges does not pretend
to be a leftist. Quite the opposite. His position in this regard leads him to sign a
petition in favor of the Bay of Pigs invaders, to call for the death penalty for
Debray, or to dedicate a book to Nixon. Many of his admirers who deplore (or
say they deplore) these acts maintain that there is a dichotomy in the man that
permits him, on the one hand, to write slightly immortal books and, on the other,
to sign political declarations that are more puerile than malicious. That may well
be. It is also possible that no such dichotomy exists and that we ought to accus-
tom ourselves to restoring unity to the author of "The Garden of Forking Paths."
By that I do not propose that we should find errors of spelling or syntax in his
elegant pages but rather that we read them for what, in the final analysis, they
are: the painful testimony of a class with no way out, diminished to saying in the
voice of one man, "The world, unfortunately, is real; I, unfortunately, am
Borges."

It is interesting that the writing/reading of Borges is enjoying a particularly
favorable reception in capitalist Europe at the moment when Europe is itself becoming a colony in the face of the "American challenge." In a book of that very
title, Jean-Jacques Servan-Schreiber explains with unmasked cynicism, "Now
then, Europe is not Algiers or Senegal!"[64] In other words, the United States can-
nont do to Europe what Europe did to Algiers and Senegal! I have bad news for
Europe: it seems that, in spite of everything, they can indeed do it; they have, in
fact, been doing it now for some time. And if this occurs in the area of econom-
ics—along with complex political derivations—the European cultural super-
structure is also manifesting obvious colonial symptoms. One of them may well
be the apogee of Borges's writing/reading.

But of course the heritage of Borges, whose kinship with Sarmiento we have
already seen, must be sought above all in Latin America, where it will imply a
further decline in impetus and quality. Since this is not a survey, but rather a simple essay on Latin-American culture, I shall restrict myself to a single example.
I am aware that it is a very minor one; but it is nonetheless a valid symptom. I
shall comment on a small book of criticism by Carlos Fuentes, *La nueva novela
hispanoamericana* [The new Spanish-American novel].

As spokesman for the same class as Borges, Fuentes also evinced leftist
whims in his younger days. The former's *El tamaño de mi esperanza* [The extent
of my hope] corresponds to the latter's *La muerte de Artemio Cruz* [The death of
Artemio Cruz]. But to continue judging Fuentes by that book, without question
one of our good novels, would be as senseless as continuing to judge Borges by
his early book—the difference being that Borges, who is more consistent (and in

all ways more estimable; Borges, even though we differ so greatly from him, is a truly important writer), decided to adopt openly his position as a man of the Right, while Fuentes operates as such but attempts to conserve, from time to time, a leftist terminology that does not lack, of course, references to Marx. In *The Death of Artemio Cruz,* a secretary who is fully integrated into the system synthesizes his biography in the following dialogue:

> "You're very young. How old are you?"
> "Twenty-seven."
> "When did you receive your degree?"
> "Three years ago. But . . . "
> "But what?"
> "Theory and practice are different."
> "And that amuses you?"
> "A lot of Marxism. So much that I even wrote my thesis on surplus value."
> "It ought to be good training, Padilla."
> "But practice is very different."
> "Is that what you are, a Marxist?"
> "Well, all my friends were. It's a stage one goes through."[65]

This dialogue expresses clearly enough the situation of a certain sector of the Mexican intelligentsia that, though it shares Borges's class circumstances and behavior patterns, differs from him for purely local reasons, in certain superficial aspects. I am thinking, specifically, of the so-called Mexican literary mafia, one of whose most conspicuous figures is Carlos Fuentes. This group warmly expressed its sympathy for the Cuban Revolution until, in 1961, the revolution proclaimed itself and proved to be Marxist-Leninist—that is, a revolution that has in its forefront a worker-peasant alliance. From that day on, the support of the mafia grew increasingly diluted, up to the last few months when—taking advantage of the wild vociferation occasioned by a Cuban writer's month in jail—they broke obstreperously with Cuba.

The symmetry here is instructive: in 1961, at the time of the Bay of Pigs, the only gathering of Latin-American writers to express in a manifesto its desire that Cuba be defeated by mercenaries in the service of imperialism was a group of Argentines centered around Borges.[66] Ten years later, in 1971, the only national circle of writers on the continent to exploit an obvious pretext for breaking with Cuba and culminating the conduct of the revolution was the Mexican mafia. It is a simple changing of the guard within an identical attitude.

In that light one can better understand the intentions of Fuentes's short book on the new Spanish-American novel. The development of this new novel is one of the prominent features of the literature of these past few years, and its circulation beyond our borders is in large part owing to the worldwide attention our continent has enjoyed since the triumph of the Cuban Revolution in 1959.[67]

Logically, this new novel has occasioned various interpretations, numerous studies. That of Carlos Fuentes, despite its brevity (less than one hundred pages), comprehends a thoroughgoing position paper on literature and politics that clearly synthesizes a shrewd rightist viewpoint within our countries.

Fuentes is quick to lay his cards on the table. In the first chapter, exemplarily entitled "Civilization and Barbarism," he adopts for openers, as might be expected, the thesis of Sarmiento: during the nineteenth century "it is possible for only one drama to unfold in this medium: that which Sarmiento established in the subtitle of *Facundo—Civilization and Barbarism.*" That drama constitutes the conflict "of the first one hundred years of Latin-American society and its novel."[68] The narrative corresponding to this conflict comprehends four factors: "an essentially alien [to whom?] natural order," which was "the real Latin-American protagonist"; the dictator on the national or regional scale; the exploited masses; and the fourth factor, "the writer, *who invariably stands on the side of civilization and against barbarism*" (11–12; my emphasis). This, according to Fuentes, implies "a defense of the exploited," but Sarmiento revealed what it consisted of in fact. The polarity that characterized the 1900s, he continued, does not go unchanged in the following century. "In the twentieth century the intellectual himself is forced to struggle within a society that is, internally and externally, much more complex,"a complexity owing to the fact that these countries will be penetrated by imperialism, while sometime later there will take place "a revolt and upsurge . . . in the underdeveloped world." Among the international factors that must be taken into account in the twentieth century, socialism, is one that Fuentes forgets to include. But he slips in this opportune formula: "We have the beginning of the transition from epic simplism to dialectical complexity" (13). "Epic simplism" was the nineteenth-century struggle in which, according to Fuentes, "the writer [he means writers *like him*] invariably stands on the side of civilization and against barbarism," that is, becomes an unconditional servant of the new oligarchy and a harsh enemy of the American masses. "Dialectical complexity" is the form that collaboration takes in the twentieth century, when the oligarchy in question has revealed itself as a mere intermediary for imperialist interests and "the writer" such as Fuentes must now serve two masters. Even when it is a question of such well-heeled masters, we have known since the Holy Scriptures that this does imply a certain "dialectical complexity," expecially when one attempts to make everyone believe one is in fact serving a third master—the people. Notwithstanding its slight omissions, the synthesis offered by the lucid Fuentes of one aspect of imperialist penetration in our countries is interesting. He writes:

In order to intervene effectively in the economic life of each

Latin-American country, it requires not only an intermediary ruling class, but a whole array of services in public administration, commerce, publicity, business management, extractive and refining industries, banking, transportation, and even entertainment: bread and circuses. General Motors assembles automobiles, takes home profits, and sponsors television programs. [14].

As a final example (even though that of General Motors is always valid) it might have been more useful to mention the CIA, which organizes the Bay of Pigs invasion and pays, via transparent intermediaries, for the review *Mundo nuevo,* one of whose principal ideologues was none other than Carlos Fuentes.

With these political premises established, Fuentes goes on to postulate certain literary premises before concentrating on the authors he will study (Vargas Llosa, Carpentier, García Márquez, Cortázar, and Goytisolo) and concluding with more observations of a political nature. I am not interested in lingering over his criticism per se but simply in underscoring a few of its ideological lines, which are, in any case, apparent: at times, this little book seems a thoroughgoing ideological manifest.

A critical appreciation of literature requires that we start off with a concept of criticism itself; one ought to have answered the elemental question, What is criticism? The modest opinion of Krystina Pomorska would seem acceptable. According to Tzvetan Todorov,

. . . she defends the following thesis: every critical method is a generalization upon the literary practice of its time. Critical methods in the period of classicism were elaborated as a function of classical literary works. The criticism of the romantics reiterates the principles (the irrational, the psychological, etc.) of romanticism itself.[69]

Reading Fuentes's criticism on the new Spanish-American novel, then, we are aware that his "critical method is a generalization upon the literary practice of its time"—the practice of *other* literatures, that is, *not* the Spanish-American. All things considered, this fits in perfectly with the alienated and alienating ideology of Fuentes.

After the work of men like Alejo Carpentier, whom some profiteers of the "boom" have tried in vain to disclaim, the undertaking assumed by the new Spanish-American novel—an undertaking that, as certain critics do not cease to observe, might appear accomplished by now or "surpassed" in the narrative of capitalist countries—implies a reinterpretation of our history. Indifferent to this incontestable fact—which in many cases bears an ostensible relationship to the new perspectives the revolution has afforded our America and which is in no small way responsible for the diffusion of our narrative among those with a desire to know the continent about which there is so much discussion—Fuentes dissipates the flesh and blood of our novels, the criticism of which would require, before anything else, understanding and evaluation of the vision of history presented in them, and, as I have said, calmly applies to the schemes derived from other literatures (those of capitalist countries), now reduced to mere linguistic speculations.

The extraordinary vogue enjoyed by linguistics in recent years has moved more than one person to conclude that "the twentieth century, which is the century of so many things, would seem to be above all the century of linguistics."[70] We, in contrast, would say that, among those "many things," the establishment of socialist governments and decolonization carry much more weight as outstanding features of this century. I might add as a modest personal example of this vogue that as recently as 1955, when I was a student of linguistics under André Martinet, linguistic matters were confined in Paris to university lecture halls. Outside the classroom we talked with our friends about literature, philosophy, and politics. Only a few years later, linguistics — whose structuralist dimension, as Lévi-Strauss described it, encompasses the other social sciences — was in Paris the obligatory theme of all discussions. In those days literature, philosopphy, and politics all ran afoul of structuralists. (I am speaking of some years ago; presently, structuralism seems to be on the decline. However, in our part of the world the insistence on such an ideology will last for sometime yet.)

Now I have no doubt that there exist specifically scientific factors to which we can credit this vogue of linguistics. But I also know that there are *ideological* reasons for it over and above the subject matter itself. With respect to literary studies it is not difficult to determine these ideological reasons. Indeed, the virtues and limitations of critical strategies ranging from Russian formalism to French structuralism cannot be shown without them. And among them is the attempt at ahistorization peculiar to a dying class: a class that initiated its trajectory with daring *utopias* in order to chase away time and that endeavors now, in the face of adversity, to arrest that trajectory via impossible *uchronics*. In any case, one must recognize the convergence between these studies and their respective conterminous literature. However, when Fuentes glosses over the concrete reality of the current Spanish-American novel and attempts to impose upon it systems derived from other literatures and other critical methodologies, he adds — with a typically colonial attitude — a second level of ideolization to his critical outlook. In a word, this is summed up in his claim that our present-day narrative — *like that of apparently coetaneous capitalist countries* — is above all a feat of language. Such a contention, among other things, allows him to minimize nicely everything in that narrative having to do with a clear historical concretion. Furthermore, the manner in which he lays the foundations of his linguistic approach demonstrates a pedantry and a provincialism typical of the colonial wishing to demonstrate to those in the metropolis that he too is capable of grappling with fashionable themes namely, themes *from abroad* — and wishing at the same time

to enlighten his fellow countrymen, in whom he is confident of finding an ignorance even greater than his own. This is the sort of thing he spews forth:

> Change comprehends the categories of process and speech, of
> diachrony; structure comprehends those of system and language, of
> synchrony. The point of interaction for all these categories is the word —
> which joins diachrony and synchrony, speech and language through
> discourse; along with process and system, through the event, and even
> event and discourse themselves.[33]

These banalities (which any handy little linguistics manual could have taken care
of), nonetheless should arouse in us more than a smile. Fuentes is elaborating as
best he can here a consistent vision of our literature, of our culture — a vision
that, significantly, coincides in its essentials with that proposed by writers like
Emir Rodríguez Monegal and Severo Sarduy.

It is revealing that for Fuentes the thesis of the preponderant role of language
in the new Spanish-American novel finds its basis in the prose of Borges,
"without which there would simply not exist a modern Spanish-American
novel," since, according to Fuentes, "the ultimate significance" of that prose is
"to bear witness, first off, that Latin America is lacking a language and must
therefore establish one." This singular triumph is achieved by Borges, Fuentes
continued, "in his creation of a new Latin-American language, which, by pure
contrast, reveals the lie, the acquiescence and the duplicity, of what has traditionally passed for 'language' among us" (26).

Naturally, based on such criteria the ahistorization of literature can attain truly
delirious expressions. We learn, for example, that Witold Gombrowicz's *Pornog-
raphy*

> could have been related by a native of the Amazon jungles and that
> neither nationality nor social class, in the final analysis, explain the
> difference between Gombrowicz and the possible narrator of the same
> initiation myth in a Brazilian jungle. Rather, it is explained precisely by
> the possibility of combining discourse in different ways. Only on the
> basis of the universality of linguistic structures can there be conceded, a
> posteriori, the peripheral data regarding nationality and class. [22]

And consequently, we are told as well that "it is closer to the truth, in the first
instance, to understand the conflict in Spanish-American literature *as related to
certain characteristics of the literary endeavor*" (24; my emphasis), rather than
to history; furthermore:

> The *old* obligation to denounce is transformed into a *much more
> arduous* enterprise: the critical elaboration of everything that has gone
> unspoken in our long history of lies, silences, rhetoric, and academic

complicities. *To invent a language is to articulate all that history has concealed.* [30; my emphasis]

Such an interpretation, then, allows Fuentes to have his cake and eat it too. Thus conceived, literature not only withdraws from any combatant role (here degraded by a clever adjective: "the *old* obligation to denounce"), but its withdrawal, far from being a retreat, becomes a *"much more arduous* enterprise," since it is to articulate no less than *"all that history has concealed."* Further on we are told that our true language is in the process of being discovered and created and that "in the very act of discovery and creation it threatens, *in a revolutionary way,* the whole economic, political, and social structure erected upon a vertically false language" (94–95; my emphasis).

This shrewd, while at the same time superficial, manner of expounding right-wing concerns in left-wing terminology reminds us — though it is difficult to forget for a single moment — that Fuentes is a member of the Mexican literary mafia, the qualities of which he has attempted to extend beyond the borders of his country.

Furthermore, that these arguments constitute the projection onto literary questions of an inherently reactionary political platform is not conjecture. This is said throughout the little book and is particularly explicit in its final pages. Besides the well-known attacks on socialism, there are observations like this one: "Perhaps the sad, immediate future of Latin America will see fascist populism, a Peronist sort of dictatorship, capable of carrying out various reforms only in exchange for a suppression of revolutionary impulse and civil liberties" (96). The "civilization vs. barbarism" thesis appears not to have changed in the least. But in fact it has — it has been agravated by the devastating presence of imperialism in our countries. In response to this reality, Fuentes erects a scarecrow: the announcement that there is opening before us

a prospect even more grave. That is, in proportion to the widening of
the abyss between the geometric expansion of the technocratic world
and the arithmetic expansion of our own ancillary societies, Latin
America is being transformed into a world that is *superfluous* [Fuentes's
emphasis] to imperialism. Traditionally we have been exploited
countries. *Soon we will not even be that* [my emphasis]. It will no
longer be necessary to exploit us, for technology will have succeeded
in — to a large extent it can already — manufacturing substitutes for our
single-product offerings.[96]

In light of this, and recalling that for Fuentes the revolution has no prospects in Latin America — he insists upon the impossibility of a "second Cuba" (96) and cannot accept the varied, unpredictable forms the process will assume — we should almost be thankful that we are not *"superfluous"* to imperialist technology, that it is not manufacturing substitutes (as *"it can already"*) for our poor products.

I have lingered perhaps longer than necessary on Fuentes because he is one of the most outstanding figures among the new Latin-American writers who have set out to elaborate in the cultural sphere a counterrevolutionary platform that, at least on the surface, goes beyond the coarse simplifications of the program "Appointment with Cuba," broadcast by the Voice of (the United States of) America. But the writers in question already had an adequate medium: the review *Mundo Nuevo* [New World], financed by the CIA,[71] whose ideological foundations are summed up by Fuentes's short book in a manner that the professorial weightiness of Emir Rodríguez Monegal or the neo-Barthean flutterings of Severo Sarduy — the magazine's other two "critics" — would have found difficult to achieve. That publication, which also gathered together the likes of Guillermo Cabrera Infante and Juan Goytisolo, is to be replaced shortly by another, which will apparently rely upon more or less the same team, along with a few additions. I am speaking of the review *Libre* [Free]. A fusion of the two titles speaks for itself: *Mundo Libre* [Free World].

The Future Begun

The endeavor to include ourselves in the "free world" — the hilarious name that capitalist countries today apply to themselves and bestow in passing on their oppressed colonies and neo-colonies — is a modern version of the nineteenth-century attempt by Creole exploiting classes to subject us to a supposed "civilization"; and this latter, in its turn, is a repetition of the designs of European conquistadors. In all these cases, with only slight variations, it is plain that Latin America does not exist except, at the very most, as a *resistance* that must be overcome in order to implant *true* culture, that of "the modern peoples who gratify themselves with the epithet of civilized."[72] Pareto's words here recall so well those of Martí, who wrote in 1883 of civilization as "the vulgar name under which contemporary European man operates."

In the face of what the conquistadores, the Creole oligarchs, and the imperialists and their flunkies have attempted, our culture — taking this term in its broad historical and anthropological sense — has been in a constant process of formation: our authentic culture, the culture created by the mestizo populace, those descendants of Indians and blacks and Europeans whom Bolívar and Artigas led so well; the culture of the exploited classes, of the radical petite bourgeoisie of José Martí, of the poor peasantry of Emiliano Zapata, of the working class of Luis Emilio Recabarren and Jesús Menéndez; the culture "of the hungry Indian masses, of the landless peasants, of the exploited workers" mentioned in the *Second Declaration of Havana* (1962), "of the honest and brilliant intellectuals who abound in our suffering Latin-American countries''; the culture of a people that now encompasses ''a family numbering two hundred million brothers'' and that ''has said: Enough! and has begun to move.''

That culture—like every living culture, especially at its dawn—*is* on the move. It has, of course, its own distinguishing characteristics, even though it was born—like every culture, although in this case in a particularly planetary way— of a synthesis. And it does not limit itself in the least to a mere repetition of the elements that formed it. This is something that the Mexican Alfonso Reyes, though he directed his attention to Europe more often than we would have wished, has underscored well. On speaking with another Latin American about the characterization of our culture as one of synthesis, he says:

> Neither he nor I were understood by our European collegues, who
> thought we were referring to the résumé or elemental compendium of
> the European conquests. According to such a facile interpretation, the
> synthesis would be a terminal point. But that is not the case: here the
> synthesis is the new point of departure, a structure composed of prior
> and dispersed elements that—like all structures—transcends them and
> contains in itself new qualities. H_2O is not only a union of hydrogen
> and oxygen; it is, moreover, water.[73]

This is especially apparent if we consider that the ''water'' in question is formed not only from European elements, which are those Reyes emphasizes, but also from the indigenous and the African. But even with his limitations, it is still within Reyes's capacity to state at the end of that piece:

> I say now before the tribunal of international thinkers within reach of
> my voice: we recognize the right to universal citizenship which we have
> won. We have arrived at our majority. Very soon you will become used
> to reckoning with us. [74]

These words were spoken in 1936. Today that ''very soon'' has already arrived. If we were asked to indicate the date that separates Reyes's hope from our certainty—considering the usual difficulties in that sort of thing—I would say 1959, the year the Cuban Revolution triumphed. One could also go along marking some of the dates that are milestones in the advent of that culture. The first, relating to the indigenous peoples' resistance and black slave revolts against European oppression, are imprecise. The year 1780 is important: it maks the uprising of Túpac Amaru in Peru. In 1803, the independence of Haiti. In 1810, the beginning of revolutionary movements in various Spanish colonies in America— movements extending well into the century. In 1867, the victory of Juárez over Maximilian. In 1895, the beginning of the final stage of Cuba's war against Spain—a war that Martí foresaw as an action against emerging Yankee imperialism. In 1910, the Mexican Revolution. In the 1920s and 1930s, Sandino's resistance in Nicaragua and the establishment on the continent of the working class as a vanguard force. In 1938, the nationalization of Mexican petroleum by Cárdenas. In 1944, the coming to power of a democratic regime in Guatemala, which was to be radicalized in office. In 1946, the beginning of Juan Domingo Perón's presidency in Argentina, under which the "shirtless ones" would become an influential force. In 1952, the Bolivian revolution. In 1959, the triumph of the Cuban Revolution. In 1961, the Bay of Pigs: the first military defeat of Yankee imperialism in America, and the declaration of our revolution as Marxist-Leninist. In 1967, the fall of Che Guevara while leading a nascent Latin-American army in Bolivia. In 1970, the election of socialist president Salvador Allende in Chile.

These dates, seen superficially, might not appear to have a very direct relationship to our culture. But, in fact, the opposite is true. Our culture is—and can only be—the child of revolution, of our multisecular rejection of all colonialisms. Our culture, like every culture, requires as a primary condition our own existence. I cannot help but cite here, although I have done so before elsewhere, one of the occasions on which Martí spoke to this fact in the most simple and illuminating way. "Letters, which are expression, cannot exist," he wrote in 1881, "so long as there is no essence to express in them. Nor will there exist a Spanish-American literature until Spanish America exists." And further: "Let us lament now that we are without a great work of art; not because we do not have that work but because it is a sign that we are still without a great people that would be reflected in it."[75] Latin-American culture, then, has become a possibility *in the first place* because of the many who have struggled, the many who still struggle, for the existence of that "great people" that in 1881, Martí still referred to as Spanish America but that some years later he would prefer to name, more accurately, "Our America."

But this is not, of course, the only culture forged here. There is also the culture of anti-America, that of the oppressors, of those who tried (or are trying) to impose on these lands metropolitan schemes, or simply, tamely to reproduce in a provincial fashion what might have authenticity in other countries. In the best of cases, to repeat, it is a question of the influence of

> those who have worked, in some cases patriotically, to shape social life
> in accordance with models of other highly developed countries, whose
> practices are the result of an organic process over the course of centuries
> [and thus] have betrayed the cause of the true emancipation of Latin
> America.[76]

This anti-America culture is still very visible. It is still proclaimed and perpetuated in structures, works, ephemerides. But without a doubt, it is suffering the pangs of death, just like the system upon which it is based. We can and must contribute to a true assessment of the history of the oppressors and that of the oppressed. But of course, the triumph of the latter will be the work, above all, of those for whom history is a function not of erudition but of deeds. It is they who will achieve the definitive triumph of the true America, reestablishing—this time in a different light—the unity of our immense continent. "Spanish America, Latin America—call it what you wish,"wrote Mariátegui,

> will not find its unity in the bourgeois order. That order divides us, perforce, into petty nationalisms. It is for Anglo-Saxon North America to consummate and draw to a close capitalist civilization. The future of Latin America is socialist.[77]

Such a future, which has already begun, will end by rendering incomprehensible the idle question about our existence.

And Ariel Now?

The Ariel of Shakespeare's great myth, which we have been following in these notes, is, as has been said, the intellectual from the same island as Caliban.[78] He can choose between serving Prospero—the case with intellectuals of the anti-American persuasion—at which he is apparently unusually adept but for whom he is nothing more than a timorous slave, or allying himself with Caliban in his struggle for true freedom. It could be said that I am thinking, in Gramscian terms, above all of the "traditional" intellectuals: those whom the proletariat, even during the period of transition, must assimilate in the greatest possible number while it generates its own "organic" intellectuals.

It is common knowledge, of course, that a more or less important segment of intellectuals at the service of the exploited classes usually comes from the exploiting classes, with which they have broken radically. This is the classic, to say the least, case of such supreme figures as Marx, Engels, and Lenin. The fact had been observed already in *The Communist Manifesto* (1848) itself, where Marx and Engels wrote:

> In times when the class struggle nears the decisive hour, the process of dissolution going on within the ruling class, in fact, within the whole range of old society, assumes such a violent, glaring character, that a small section of the ruling class cuts itself adrift and joins the revolutionary class, the class that holds the future in its hands . . . [S]o now a portion of the bourgeoisie goes over to the proletariat and, in particular, a portion of the bourgeois ideologists, who have raised themselves to the level of comprehending theoretically the historical movement as a whole.[79]

If this is obviously valid with regard to the most highly developed capitalist nations—the ones Marx and Engels had in mind in the *Manifesto*—something more must be added in the case of our countries. Here that "portion of the bourgeois ideologists" to which Marx and Engels refer experiences a second form of rupture: except for that sector proceeding organically from the exploited classes, the intelligentsia that considers itself revolutionary must break all ties with its class of origin (frequently the petite bourgeoisie) and must besides sever the nexus of *dependence* upon the metropolitan culture from which it has learned, nonetheless, a language as well as a conceptual and technical apparatus.[80] That language will be of profit, to use Shakespearean terminology, in cursing Prospero. Such was the case with José María Heredia, who exclaimed in the finest Spanish of the first third of the nineteenth century, "The vilest of traitors might serve him,/ But the tyrant's passion is all in vain./ For the sea's immense and rolling waves/ Span the distance from Cuba to Spain." It was also the case of José Martí. After spending fifteen years in the United States—which would allow him to become completely familiar with modernity and to detect within that country the emergence of North American imperialism—he wrote: "I have lived in the monster, and I know its entrails; and my sling is the sling of David." While I can foresee that my suggestion that Heredia and Martí went about cursing will have an unpleasant ring in the ears of some, I wish to remind them that "vile traitors" and "monster" do have something to do with curses. Both Shakespeare and reality would appear to argue well against their objection. And Heredia and Martí are only archetypal examples. More recently we have not been lacking either in individuals who attribute the volcanic violence in some of Fidel's recent speeches to deformations—Caliban, let us not forget, is always seen as deformed by the hostile eye—in our revolution. Response to his address at the first National Congress on Education and Culture is one example of this. That some of those shocked should have praised Fanon (others, perhaps had never heard of him, since they have as much to do with politics, in the words of Rodolfo Walsh, as with astrophysics), and now attribute an attitude that is at the very root of our historical being to a deformation or to foreign influence, might be a sign of any number of things—among them, total incoherence. It might also be a question of total ignorance, if not disdain, regarding our concrete realities, past and present. This, most assuredly, does not qualify them to have very much to do with our future.

The situation and tasks of the intellectual in the service of the exploited classes differ, of course, depending upon whether it is a question of a country where the revolution has yet to triumph or one where the revolution is already underway. And, as we have recalled above, the term "intellectual" is broad enough to counter any attempts at simplification. The intellectual can be a theoretician and leader like Mariátegui or Mella; a scholar, like Fernando Ortiz; or a writer like César Vallejo. In all these cases their concrete example is more instructive than any vague generalization.[81]

The situation, as I said, is different in countries where the Latin-American masses have at last achieved power and set in motion a socialist revolution. The encouraging case of Chile is too immediate to allow for any conclusions to be drawn. But the socialist revolution in Cuba is more than twelve years old, and by this time it is possible to point out certain facts — although, owing to the nature of this essay, I propose to mention here only a few salient characteristics.

This revolution — in both practice and theory absolutely faithful to the most exacting popular Latin-American tradition — has satisfied in full the aspiration of Mariátegui. "We certainly do not wish for socialism in Latin American to be a carbon copy," he said. "It must be a heroic creation. With our own reality, in our own language, we must give life to Indo-American socialism."[82]

That is why our revolution cannot be understood without a knowledge of "our own reality," "our own language," and to these I have referred extensively. But the unavoidable pride in having inherited the best of Latin-American history, in struggling in the front ranks of a family numbering 200 million brothers and sisters, must not cause us to forget that as a consequence we form part of another even larger vanguard, a planetary vanguard — that of the socialist countries emerging on every continent. This means that our inheritance is also the worldwide inheritance of socialism and that we commit ourselves to it as the most beautiful, the most lofty, the most combative chapter in the history of humanity. We feel as unequivocally our own socialism's past: from the dreams of the utopian socialists to the impassioned scientific rigor of Marx ("That German of tender spirit and iron hand," as Martí said) and Engels, from the heroic endeavor of the Paris Commune of a century ago to the startling triumph of the October Revolution and the abiding example of Lenin, from the establishment of new socialist governments in Europe as a result of the defeat of fascism in World War II to the success of socialist revolutions in such "underdeveloped" Asian countries as China, Korea, and Vietnam. When we affirm our commitment to such a magnificent inheritance — one that we aspire besides to enrich with our own contributions — we are well aware that this quite naturally entails shining moments as well as difficult ones, achievements as well as errors. How could we not be aware of this when on making *our own* history (an operation that has nothing to do with *reading* the history of others), we find ourselves also subject to achievements and errors, just as all *real* historical movements have been and will continue to be!

This elemental fact is constantly being recalled, not only by our declared enemies but even by some supposed friends, whose only apparent objection to socialism is, at bottom, that it exists — in all its grandeur and with its difficulties, in spite of the flawlessness with which this written swan appears in books. We cannot but ask ourselves why we should go on offering explanations to those supposed friends about the problems we face in *real-life* socialist construction, especially when their consciences allow them to remain integrated into exploiting societies or, in some cases, even to abandon our neocolonial countries and request, hat in hand, a place in those very societies. No, there is no reason to give any explanation to that sort of people, who, were they honest, should be concerned about having so much in common with our enemies. The frivolous way in which some intellectuals who call themselves leftists (and who, nonetheless, don't seem to give a damn about the masses) rush forth shamelessly to repeat word for word the same critiques of the socialist world proposed and promulgated by capitalism only demonstrates that they have not broken with capitalism as radically as they might perhaps think. The natural consequence of this attitude is that under the guise of rejecting error (something upon which any opposing factions can come to an agreement), socialism as a whole, reduced arbitrarily to such errors, is rejected in passing; or there is the deformation and generalization of a concrete historical moment and, extracting it from its context, the attempt to apply it to other historical moments that have *their own characteristics, their own virtues, and their own defects.* This is one of the many things that, in Cuba, we have learned in the flesh.

During these years, in search of original and above all *genuine* solutions to our problems, an extensive dialogue on cultural questions has taken place in Cuba. *Casa de las Américas,* in particular, has published a number of contributions to the dialogue. I am thinking particularly of the round table in which I participated, with a group of colleagues, in 1969.[83]

And, of course, the leaders of the revolution themselves have not been remiss in expressing opinions on these matters. Even though, as Fidel has said, "we did not have our Yenan Conference" before the triumph of the revolution,[84] since that time discussions, meetings, and congresses designed to grapple with these questions have taken place. I shall limit myself to recalling a few of the many texts by Fidel and Che. Regarding the former, there is his speech at the National Library of 30 June 1961, published that year and known since then as *Words to the Intellectuals;* his speech of 13 March 1969 in which he dealt with the democratization of the university and to which we referred a number of times in the above-mentioned round table; and finally, his contribution to the recent Congress on Education and Culture, which we published, together with the declaration of the congress, in number 65–66 of *Casa de las Américas.* Of course, these are not by any means the only occasions on which Fidel has taken up cultural problems, but I think they offer a sufficiently clear picture of the revolution's pertinent criteria.

Although a decade has passed between the first of these speeches—which I am convinced has scarcely been read by many of its commentators, who limit themselves to quoting the odd sentence or two out of context—and the most recent one, what an *authentic* reading of both demonstrates above all is a consistency over the ten-year period. In 1971, Fidel has this to say about literary and other artistic works:

> We, a revolutionary people, value cultural and artistic creations in
> proportion to what they offer mankind, in proportion to their

contribution to the revindication of man, the liberation of man, the happiness of man . . . Our evaluation is political. There can be no aesthetic value in opposition to man. Aesthetic value cannot exist in opposition to justice, in opposition to the welfare or in opposition to the happiness of man. It cannot exist!

In 1961, he had declared:

It is man himself, his fellow man, the redemption of his fellow man that constitutes the objective of the revolutionary. If they ask us revolutionaries what matters most to us, we say the people, and we will always say the people. The people in the truest sense, that is, the majority of the people, those who have had to live in exploitation and in the cruelest neglect. Our basic concern will always be the great majority of the people, that is, the oppressed and exploted classes. The prism through which we see everything is this: whatever is good for them will be good for us; whatever is noble, useful, and beautiful for them will be noble, useful, and beautiful for us.

And those words of 1961, so often cited out of context, must be returned to that context for a full understanding of their meaning:

Within the revolution, everything; outside the revolution, nothing. Outside the revolution, nothing, because the revolution also has its rights; and the first right of the revolution is to be, to exist. No one, to the extent that the revolution understands the interests of the people, to the extent that the revolution expresses the interest of the nation as a whole, can maintain any right in opposition to it.

But consistency is not repetition. The correspondence between the two speeches does not mean that the past ten years have gone by in vain. At the beginning of his *Words to the Intellectuals* Fidel had recalled that the economic and social revolution taking place in Cuba was bound inevitably to produce in its turn a revolution in the culture of our country. The decisions proclaimed in the 1969 speech on the democratization of the university along with those of the 1971 speech at the National Congress on Education and Culture correspond, among other things, to the very transformation mentioned already in 1961 as an outcome of the economic and social revolution. During those ten years there has been taking place an uninterrupted radicalization of the revolution, which implies a growing participation of the masses in the country's destiny. If the agrarian reform of 1959 will be followed by an agrarian revolution, the literacy campaign will inspire a campaign for follow-up courses, and the later announcement of the democratization of the university already supposes that the masses have conquered the domains of so-called high culture. Meanwhile, in a parallel way, the process of syndical democratization brings about an inexorable growth in the role played by the working class in the life of the country.

In 1961 this could not yet have been the case. In that year the literacy campaign was only just being carried out. The foundations of a truly new culture were barely being laid. By now, 1971, a great step forward has been taken in the development of that culture; a step already foreseen in 1961, one involving tasks that must inevitably be accomplished by any revolution that calls itself socialist: the extension of education to all of the people, its firm grounding in revolutionary principles, and the construction and safeguarding of a new, socialist culture.

To better understand the goals as well as the specific characteristics of *our* developing cultural transformation, it is useful to compare it to similar processes in other socialist countries. The creation of conditions by which an entire people who have lived in exploitation and illiteracy gains access to the highest levels of knowledge and creativity is one of the most beautiful achievements of a revolution.

Cultural questions also engaged a good part of Ernesto Che Guevara's attention. His study, *El socialismo y el hombre en Cuba* [Man and Socialism in Cuba], is sufficiently well known to make comment on it unnecessary here. But the reader should be warned, above all, against following the example of those who take him a la carte, selecting, for example, his censure of a certain conception of a socialist realism but not his censure of decadent art under modern capitalism and its continuation in our society—or vice versa.[85] Or who forget with what astonishing clarity he foresaw certain problems of our artistic life, expressing himself in terms that on being taken up again by pens less prestigious than his own, would raise objections no one dared make to Che himself.

Because it is less known than *Man and Socialism in Cuba,* I would like to close by citing at some length the end of a speech delivered by Che at the University of Las Villas on 28 December 1959, that is, at the very beginning our our revolution. The university had made him professor *honoris causa* in the School of Pedagogy, and Che's speech was to express his gratitude for the distinction. He did so, but what he did above all was to propose to the university, to its professors and students, a transformation that all of them—and us—would have to undergo in order to be considered truly revolutionary, truly useful:

> I would never think of demanding that the distinguished professors or
> the students presently associated with the University of Las Villas
> perform the miracle of admitting to the university the masses of workers
> and peasants. The road here is long; it is a process all of you have lived
> through, one entailing many years of preparatory study. What I do ask,
> based on my own limited experience as a revolutionary and rebel
> commandante, is that the present students of the University of Las Villas
> understand that study is the patrimony of no one and that the place of
> study where you carry out your work is the patrimony of no one—it

belongs to all the people of Cuba, and it must be extended to the people
or the people will seize it. And I would hope—because I began the
whole series of ups and downs in my career as a university student, as a
member of the middle class, as a doctor with middle-class perspectives
and the same youthful aspirations that you must have, and because I
have changed in the course of the struggle, because I am convinced of
the overwhelming necessity of the revolution and the infinite justice of
the people's cause—I would hope for those reasons that you, today
proprietors of the university, will extend it to the people. I do not say
this as a threat, so as to avoid its being taken over by them tomorrow. I
say it simply because it would be one more among so many beautiful
examples in Cuba today: that the proprietors of the Central University of
Las Villas, the students, offer it to the people through their
revolutionary government. And to the distinguished professors, my
colleagues, I have to say something similar: become black, mulatto, a
worker, a peasant; go down among the people, respond to the people,
that is, to all the necessities of all of Cuba. When this is accomplished,
no one will be the loser; we all will have gained, and Cuba can then
continue its march toward the future with a more vigorous step, and you
will not need to include in your cloister this doctor, commandante, bank
president, and today professor of pedagogy who now takes leave of
you.[86]

That is to say, Che proposed that the "European university," as Martí would have
said, yield before the "American university." He proposed to Ariel, through his
own most luminous and sublime example if ever there was one, that he seek from
Caliban the honor of a place in his rebellious and glorious ranks.

—Havana, 7–20 June 1971
—Translated by Lynn Garafola,
David Arthur McMurray, and Roberto Márquez

Caliban Revisited

Nineteen eighty-five was the 240th anniversary of Jonathan Swift's death. There are those who have said that he died an idiot or, at very least, afflicted with a severe psychic disorder. I don't know if this is so; reading biographies and histories of people and things familiar to me has made me suspect what some people have said about them. In any event, it was surely prior to that supposed disorder that he wrote his superb and well-known epitaph, which begins, "Iit ubi saeva indignatio ulterius cor lacerari nequit," and concludes, "Abi, viator, et imitare, si poteris, strenuum pro virili libertatis vindicatorem." Thus, in 1745, he departed to a place where savage indignation could no longer wound the heart of a man who justly considered himself worthy of daring the traveler to emulate, if at all possible, his labors in the cause of human liberty. Swift performed this task in a variegated and mordant literary oeuvre that is read today far less than it deserves—with a single exception, *Gulliver's Travels* (1726).[1] This book is also a tremendous lesson to writers, for the ardent pamphleteer who earned the praise of men whom I admire—such as George Bernard Shaw and Bertolt Brecht—who tirelessly flayed humanity's foibles, has gone down in history as a harmless teller of children's tales.[2] His tiger, not unworthy of Blake's, has been turned into a meek tabby for the delight of tiny readers. And yet that book was born of the author's savage indignation, as was nearly everything he wrote. Unexpectedly, he teaches us an important lesson with this metamorphosis. It isn't a new lesson, much less a unique one, but in his case it takes on a shattering dimension: a text, beyond not merely the author's intent (which often is unknowable) but his context as well, can turn into something quite different from what it was, from what it is.

I have allowed myself this grand reminder in the face of a rather small fact: my essay, "Caliban," soon will turn fifteen. Since it was first published in the pages of the Cuban journal *Casa de las Américas* (no. 68, September—October 1971), it has gone through numerous editions both in its original language and in translation. It has also been the object of not a few commentaries. The diverse nature of the latter and the fact that the former is again seeing the light of day a decade and a half after its birth, leads me to visit it once more. I still feel grateful for some of those commentaries. Others, as is often the case, I consider mistaken. But what I find most striking is that, torn from its context, with the best of intentions in some instances and the worst in others, my own essay has at times seemed to me virtually unrecognizable. Unless it is restored to the context in which it was written, it runs the risk of turning into gibberish. This is why I have no choice but to recall, albeit in general terms, the circumstance of its birth. I shall try to do so.

I'm not much given to the division of history into decades, which English-speaking people so love, but at times it seems inevitable, just as the division into centuries is inevitable. The trouble is that we might take such divisions too seriously and imagine, for example, that on 1 January 1900 or 1 January 2000 something definitively new began or will begin. Nonetheless, with all due caution, both decades and centuries can have their uses. I would like, as a case in point, to call attention to a noteworthy book, *The 60s Without Apology*.[3]

Armed with these precautions, it would be well to bear in mind that "Caliban" came out in 1971: at the juncture between the sixties, which had just ended, and the seventies, which had just begun. I wish to evoke the earlier of the two decades, as in the aforementioned book, without apology—and without nostalgia, either, because there will always be new and necessary battles. It was a beautiful moment when intellectual life in many countries was under the hegemony of the Left: just as, the moment when I am writing, it is in not a few capitalist countries, regrettably under the hegemony of the Right. It is no accident that in many of those countries there is talk of a new Right, while in others, a similar situation takes the form of an apparent depoliticization. All the more reason, I might add, to hold in esteem those who, in these circumstances, bravely hold to their positions. The beautiful Sandinista Revolution of Nicaragua, when it triumphed in 1979, did so in this atmosphere, which, nonetheless, will not hinder the forces of democracy from preventing an act of direct imperialist agression against the homeland of Rubén Darío.

The year before the decade of the sixties began, the Cuban Revolution had taken power. Its repercussions are far from having been dissipated, but they were felt especially strongly in that decade. And the sixties witnessed, among other things, the triumph of the Algerian Revolution and the dramatic Vietnam War, which would come to an end considerably later: these are events that would strongly influence the respective metropolises. The Right saw movements of oppressed "races" and communities, of women, of marginal peoples, develop before their very eyes. There was, naturally, no lack of absurdity, like the hippies and flower power. In our America, the certainty of victory of guerrilla movements of broadly socialist orientation took root in many hearts and became incarnate in innumerable acts of heroism. Many figures remained as milestones along the road of these hopes, the most heraldic of which, no doubt, is Che. In our America, too, literature, lead but not overwhelmed by the novel, stood at the foreground of the world stage, followed in close proximity by the new cinema and music. At the dawn of the next decade, in 1970, the socialist Salvador Allende was elected president of Chile.

Of course imperialism was not (and never is) an idle spectator. While politically it undertook a variety of operations—ranging from aggression against Cuba to the occupation of the Dominican Republic, from the organization of counterinsurgency and the establishment of new tyrannies to the Alliance for Progress—intellectually it plotted an academic version of its demagogic policy. (At the time of the Second World War, this version was graphically exemplified by a well-known Walt Disney movie, in homage to that movie, this version might have been called *Saludos, amigos escritores y artistas latinoamericanos* [Greetings, Latin-American Writer and Artist Friends].) Grants proliferated, colloquiums flourished, chairs to study and dissect us sprouted like toadstools after a rainstorm. There was even talk, in the most wretched stock-market taste, of the "boom" of the Latin-American novel. It would be unjust to attribute all this to malevolence; many Western intellectuals and institutions evinced a serious attitude toward the emerging realities of what until then had been relegated to the outskirts of history. This new seriousness grew within the framework of real attention to what the French demographer Alfred Sauvy had already, in 1952, baptized "the Third World". The manifest disdain toward 'Third World-ism' being voiced these days in so many openly reactionary quarters (and in others that echo them, as the spectrum slides to the Right) cannot make us forget that concern for colonial and formerly colonial countries implied, and in many instances still implies, a genuine interest without which it is not possible to understand the world we live in today.

At the very outset of the cold war, before the Third World had not entered the ring with such intensity, the United States organized, among other operations, the Congress for Cultural Freedom, in which the crude anti-Communism of practical politicians was adorned with intellectual sighs and breast-beating.[4] In Spanish, the Congress's journal was called *Cuadernos;* its form was so sclerotic that it was unable to ride the rising tide of the sixties, and thus, it capsized ingloriously on its one hundredth issue. Shortly thereafter, the substitution of *Mundo Nuevo* for *Cuadernos* was planned and accomplished.

The debate that raged around this review permeated the atmosphere in which "Caliban" was conceived. In the mid-sixties, when the imminent publication in

Paris of the new review became known, a group of writers, myself included, called attention to the fact that *Mundo Nuevo* could do nothing more than put a better face on its predecessor and that, in essence, it would have a similar purpose. *Mundo Nuevo* was undoubtedly superior to *Cuadernos,* and it brought in a substantially new team. The project was clear: to challenge, from Europe and with a modern look, the hegemony of the revolutionary outlook in Latin-American intellectual work.[5] It would be mistaken to contend, and we never suggested, that everyone who published in *Mundo Nuevo* was necessarily hostile to the revolution. On the contrary, the editors' purpose was to create an atmosphere of confusion that would make it difficult to detect the real functions that the review had been assigned. The accusations reached new heights on 27 April 1966, when the *New York Times* published a lengthy article on the CIA's financing of the Congress for Cultural Freedom and its publications. Despite the pharisaic denials issued by the Congress's leadership and some of its contributors, on 14 May 1967, two London newspapers, the *Sunday Times* and the *Observer,* ran detailed reports that definitively clarified the question: the congress's executive secretary, Michael Josselson, admitted everything in Paris. For the *Sunday Times,* it was a "Story of a Literary Bay of Pigs." Among the Spanish-language commentaries on these events, "Epitafio para un imperio cultural" [Epitaph for a Cultural Empire], an article published in the Uruguayan weekly *Marcha* on 27 May of that year by the noted Peruvian writer Mario Vargas Llosa was particularly significant. A few years ago, in 1983, Vargas Llosa (who is now quite far from the Left) published a selection of his articles, entitled *Contra viento y marea (1962–1982)* [Against wind and tide (1962–1982)].[6] Unfortunately, in that thick book (to which we shall return) Vargas Llosa did not find space for so important an article, which concluded:

> The "cultural empire" built with such painstaking cleverness, at such expense, has collapsed like a house of cards, and the pity is that, among its smoking ruins lie, broken, dirtied, guilty and innocent, those who acted in good faith and those who did so in bad faith, those who believed that they were there to fight for freedom and those who solely were interested in picking up their pay.[7]

In its next issue (2 June 1967), *Marcha* published the succinct history, in the form of a chronological tables, of the polemics of the affair, beginning with an exchange of correspondence between the editor of *Mundo Nuevo* and myself (which was given space in a number of periodicals) and following up with further details. But to assume that the "cultural empire" had been overthrown simply because *one* of its maneuvers had been unmasked is to engage in wishful thinking. *Mundo Nuevo* disappeared after those revelations, but among all sorts of people it sowed seeds of possible distrust toward the Latin-American revolution, which at that time could offer only the victorious example of Cuba, itself virtually overwhelmed by the diverse (and even contradictory) expectations that many people had of it but limited in actuality by its meager strength and inevitable errors. In 1968 the argument over a literary prize awarded to a book written by the poet Heberto Padilla by the Unión de Escritores y Artistas de Cuba [Association of Cuban Writers and Artists] (which published the book with a prologue expressing its disagreements) gave "those who acted in good faith and those who did so in bad faith" renewed vigor. For three years, the book's author continued to work and write in Cuba. But in 1971 his month-long detention on charges of counterrevolutionary activities (*not* for the writing or publication of any poem) unleashed a broadly based argument into which were dragged, far more than ever before, men and women of good and bad faith. In addition, the move toward the Right was beginning. On the side of the Cuban Revolution's critics, the most significant event was the appearance of two open letters addressed to Fidel from Europe. The first one stated that the undersigned, despite their "solidarity with the principles and goals of the Cuban Revolution," addressed him "in order to express their concern arising from the arrest of the well-known [*sic*] poet and writer Heberto Padilla." Further down, it added:

> Given that so far the Cuban government has not provided any
> information on the matter, this fact makes us fear the reappearance of a
> process of sectarianism even stronger and more dangerous than the one
> denounced by you in March 1962. . . . At a time when a socialist
> government has taken office in Chile and a new situation created in
> Peru and Bolivia facilitates the breaking down of American
> imperialism's criminal blockade of Cuba, *the use of repressive methods*
> *against intellectuals and writers who have availed themselves of their*
> *right to criticism within the revolution* cannot but have profoundly
> negative repercussions on anti-imperialist forces throughout the world,
> and most especially in Latin America, where the Cuban Revolution is a
> symbol and banner.[8]

This letter was copiously circulated by the world's capitalist media, becoming—whatever the intentions of at least some of its signers might have been—an open accusation against the Cuban Revolution, given the letter's assumption of the "use of repressive methods," and so forth, in Cuba. But its hue paled in comparison to the second letter. Contary to what has been said even with the best of goodwill, this second letter was not the necessary consequence of the lack of response (since response would have been nearly impossible) to the first one. Between the first letter and the second stood a fiery speech by Fidel, the freeing of Padilla, and at his request, the publication of a document of self-criticism that, as became evident later on, was nothing more than a malicious caricature of the self-accusations prompted by the sadly famous Moscow trials in the mid-thirties. In other words, it was material written to be decoded by those already predisposed to seeing Cuba as undergoing a period similar to the so-called cult of personality in the USSR of the thirties.

The second letter did not have the backing of many of those who had lent their names to the first one. Among those who refused to sign the second letter, Julio Cortázar, by virtue of his conduct and his unimpeachable honesty, occupies a prominent place. In his letter dated 4 February 1972, in which he responds to one sent him by Haydée Santamaría, Cortázar said:

> as to the writing of the first letter, the one I signed, I can simply tell you this: the original text that [Juan] Goytisolo submitted to me was very similar to the text of the second letter, that is, *paternalistic, insolent, unacceptable in every regard.* I refused to sign it, and I proposed an alternate text that, respectfully, went no further than a request for information about what had happened; you'd probably reply that, in addition, it expressed concern that a kind of "sectarian squeeze" was taking place in Cuba, and that's so; we feared this might be happening, but that fear was neither betrayal nor indignation nor protest. Please, reread the text and compare it to that of the second letter, which I naturally didn't sign. I can tell you (the "Policrítica" [Polycritique] says so as well, of course) that I'm sorry that the comrade-to-comrade request for information was accompanied by that expression of concern; but I insist that *insolent interference or paternalism of the kind displayed in the second, unspeakable letter* can by no means be attributed to those who signed the first one.[9]

That second letter, deserving of Cortázar's description, stated:

> We deem it our duty to communicate to you our shame and anger. The pitiful text of the confession that Heberto Padilla signed can only have been obtained by methods that are the negation of revolutionary legality and justice. The content and form of said confession, with its absurd accusations and delirious statements, as well as the meeting that took place at UNEAC in which Padilla himself and comrades Belkis Cuza, Díaz Martínez, César López and Pablo Armando Fernández submitted to a pitiful charade of self-criticism, recalls the most sordid moments of the Stalinist period, its prefabricated practices and witch-hunts.[10] With the same vehemence with which we have defended the Cuban Revolution from the outset, because we deemed it exemplary in its respect for human beings and in its struggle for liberation, we exhort it to avoid for Cuba the dogmatic obscurantism, the cultural xenophobia and the repressive system that Stalinism imposed in the socialist countries, in which events similar to those taking place in Cuba were flagrant examples. The disregard for human dignity entailed in forcing a man ridiculously to accuse himself of the worst betrayals and the vilest acts does not alarm us because it involves a writer but because any Cuban comrade—a peasant, worker, technician or intellectual—might

also be a victim of a similar act of violence or humiliation. We would like the Cuban Revolution once more to become what at one time lead us to consider it a model within socialism.[11]

Cortázar died faithful to the ideas he expounded to Haydée in his letter of 4 February 1972. We can gather as much from the text added to a later edition of his valiant book *Nicaragua tan violentamente dulce* [Nicaragua so Violently Sweet], which, according to the colophon, "was printed on 25 January 1984," in Barcelona. (The first edition, without that essay, had appeared in Nicaragua in 1983.) The new text is titled "Apuntes al margen de una relectura de *1984*" [Marginal Notations to a Rereading of 1984]. Although he states therein that "if the Padilla case finally had any positive outcome, it was that it separated the wheat from the chaff outside Cuba," he insists on the supposed virtues of the first letter. In contrast, he calls the second one "the well-known letter *of the French intellectuals* to Fidel Castro . . . , which was *paternalistic and unpardonable in its insolence*," and he adds, "but I can state with all necessary proof that that second letter never would have been sent if the first request for information regarding the facts — which I signed along with many others — had been answered within a reasonable period of time."[12]

Plainly, when Cortázar wrote those words he had not read Mario Vargas Llosa's aforementioned book, *Contra viento y marea (1962–1982),* "printed in the month of November, 1983," according to its colophon, which makes it virtually simultaneous with Julio's. In the Peruvian's book, the second open letter to Fidel appears with the following footnote:

> The initiative for this protest was born in Barcelona, when the world press made known the UNEAC meeting in which Heberto Padilla emerged from the Cuban police dungeon to perform his "self-criticism." Juan and Luis Goytisolo, José María Castellet, Hans Magnus Enzensberger, Carlos Barral (who later decided not to sign the letter), and I got together at my house and wrote, each of us separately, a draft. Then we compared them and selected mine by vote. The poet Jaime Gil de Biedma improved the text by the addition of an adverb.[13]

Vargas Llosa therefore admits a number of things in this passage, the first being his authorship of the letter, which consequently was not the product of "French intellectuals" (proportionately there were no more of them signing this one than the first letter). Furthermore, he adds a list of sixty-one signatures, indifferent to the fact that many of the signers, just as with the previous letter, later expressed their disagreement with that course of action.

In addition to all these documents, many others, both for and against the Cuban position, appeared in numerous publications, fanning the flames of controversy. If I have brought these matters to bear, it is because they are the spark that fired the writing of "Caliban." Three successive issues of *Casa de las Américas* were devoted to the dispute. The last of them, which bore the collective title *Sobre cultura y revolución en América Latina* [On Culture and Revolution in Latin America], included my essay. If it is now disengaged from that polemic, or if that polemic is not taken into account, it is evident that the meaning of "Caliban" is betrayed. I do not demand that readers familiarize themselves with all the material that surfaced in the heat of the polemic, but rather that they recall its bitterness. My piece was not born in a vacuum but rather at a particular time that was marked by passion, and—on our part—indignation at the paternalism, the rash accusation against Cuba, and even the grotesque "shame" and "anger" of those who, comfortably situated in the "West" with their fears, their guilt, and their prejudices, decided to proclaim themselves judges of the revolution.

But I would be simplistic to suppose that it was solely these skirmishes that gave rise to my text. Beginning much earlier, spurred on by the great intellectual challenge that the revolution we were (and are) living hurled at us, I had been broaching questions that, in some fashion, prefigured the 1971 essay. It is sufficient to recall a few journalistic pieces from 1959 and the essays "El son de vuelo popular" [The People's Poetic Voice] (written in 1962, on Nicolas Guillén's poetry), "Mart en su (tercer) mundo" [1965: Martí in his (Third) World] (1965), and "Introducción al pensamiento de Che" [Introduction to Che's Thought] (1967), just to point out a few earlier stepping stones.[14] In general, it was a matter of reinterpreting our world in the demanding light of the revolution.

I will not spend an inordinate amount of time on "Caliban"'s anagrammatic history, which has been dealt with in minute detail by Roger Toumson in his book *Trois Calibans* [Three Calibans] (1981),[15] nor on whether I am an imitator of the French, as, after a lengthy silence, Emir Rodríguez Monegal, the Uruguayan critic and former editor of *Mundo Nuevo*, would have it.[16] I'm not much given to arguments with the dead, and I don't wish to deny the value of that writer's every word, but I do not believe that full immersion in cultural politics under the auspicies of imperialism did him any good. When calling me a Gallicizer, supposing as he did that my use of the symbol of Caliban had French roots (a part of my cultural training does, though, of course, it has other roots as well), he coincided, perhaps unwittingly, with a repeated accusation made by the Voice of America's "Date with Cuba" program, bringing me together with friends such as Carpentier, Pérez de la Riva and Le Riverand in a sort of archaic Spanish insult that goes back centuries. Rodríguez Monegal seemed to forget on the one hand, that Caliban was an English, not a French, character, and on the other, that it was writers from the British West Indies like George Lamming and Edward Brathwaite, both of whom are cited in my text, who first connected the character to our countries—concretely, the Caribbean.[17] Although I believe I was first to apply the symbol of Caliban to our America as a whole in Spanish, I don't think it particularly meritorious of me. In any event, Rodríguez Monegal got so interested in the subject that he didn't stop until he offered university courses on it, which I always understood as a sort of involuntary homage he rendered me.

While we're on the subject of living authors, I'd like to mention a couple: one is Jorge Luis Borges; Carlos Fuentes is another. On the first of the two, who is called in the text "a truly important writer, although we so often disagree with him, " I must state that I have never believed, as the English critic J. M. Cohen suspects in his useful book on the Argentine writer, that the prizes and distinctions he has been awarded have had anything to do with his political evolution.[18] On the contrary, I always believed, and have had the opportunity to reconfirm, that with his ironic humor, he was an honest and modest man endowed with exceptional talent, whose political compass, which in his youth lead him to praise the October Revolution and later on to defend the Spanish Republic and oppose Nazi anti-Semitism, became disoriented (like that of many other Argentinians) when Perón took the reins of government in his country. His pronouncements became delirious and, furthermore, contrary to what he himself thinks, he is a writer with a political drift, which ranges between anarchism and conservatism.[19] But his pronouncements have been toned down, and his literary quality seems to me now, looking at his work as a whole from the perspective of his very great old age, even better than it seemed to me then. Finally, I believe that the Mexican critic Jorge Alberto Manrique is quite right when, in one of the first critical notices of "Caliban," he points out:

> It would be well to remember, as Borges himself has said, that vis-á-vis . . . [the] reading of Europe, he takes the sniping stance of an ironist, "from without." The best of his work is made of that: and in it can be recognized an attitude of Caliban. For everyone has his own responses, and it's worth the trouble to try to understand them.[20]

It would not be right, on the other hand, to hide the fact that the sharpness of tone and the occasional sarcasm a propos of Fuentes took into account not only his work but, in addition, the fact that the Mexican, one of the most important Latin-American novelists of recent years, after having been politically close to us (which I would like him to continue being), was one of the main contributors to and ideologues of *Mundo Nuevo,* a signer of the two letters to Fidel in 1971, and the author of some unjust remarks on Cuba. This was the background that lead me to call the views he held back then into question in vivid terms: views that, furthermore, still seem mistaken to me. But since then, although Fuentes has not gone out of his way to insult me (rather than to argue with me), he has shown unequivocal support for the Cuban and Nicaraguan revolutions. I could not revisit my essay without saying these things, whatever the reaction to them may be.

The circumstances in which I had to write "Caliban," in a few days, practically without sleeping or eating, feeling myself pressured by people for whom I have the highest regard, are responsible for a number of loose ends in the piece that gave rise to misunderstandings. Later on, I tried to tie them up. Thus, for example, the relation between our America and its former collective metropolis lead me to write "Nuestra América y Occidente" [Our America and the West], and I dealt with the relation of Latin America to Spain in "Contra la leyenda Negra" [Against the Black Legend], which someone called my love letter to Spain. And, on a broader scale one that goes beyond regional limitations, I thought it necessary to revise "Algunos usos de civilización y barbarie" [Some Uses of Civilization and Barbarism]. In other instances, I was more concerned with literary than historical considerations. I think that the piece in that group that I least dislike is "Algunos problemas teóricos de la literatura hispanoameri-cana" [Some Theoretical Problems Concerning Latin-American Literature]. I have also touched (before and since) on problems that are less vast, more limited to particular authors or situations, but from the same viewpoint.

Caliban, then, became a crossroad where my earlier work lead and my later work began. Still, I would not like it to be judged in isolation but rather within the constellation of pieces that took shape around it. My wish is not, and never was, to present Latin America and the Caribbean as a region cut off from the rest of the world but rather to view it precisely as a part of the world—a part that should be looked at with the same attention and respect as the rest, not as a merely paraphrastic expression of the West. Several friends did me the honor of pointing out similarities between my goal, dealing with our reality, and the one the Palestinian Edward W. Said had set for himself in his noteworthy book Orientalism (1978).[21]

If there is one thing that troubles me now about the term "Third World," it is the degradation that it perhaps involuntarily presupposes. There is just one world in which the oppressors and the oppressed struggle, one world in which, rather sooner than later, the oppressed will be victorious. Our America is bringing its own nuances to this struggle, this victory. The tempest has not subsided. But The Tempest's shipwrecked sailors, Crusoe and Gulliver, can be seen, rising out of the waters, from terra firma. There, not only Prospero, Ariel and Caliban, Don Quixote, Friday and Faust await them, but Sofía and Oliveira, and Colonel Aureliano Buendía as well, and—halfway betwen history and dream—Marx and Lenin, Bolívar and Martí, Sandino and Che Guevara.

—Havana, 13 March 1986

Against the Black Legend

To my Spanish comrades,
in and outside Spain

The Paleo-Western Heritage

The stimulating discussion, renewed in recent years, on the nature of Latin-American culture has come to emphasize the authenticity of our indigenous Indo-American and African heritage and to point out our distance from—or, if you will, our sympathies with and differences from—the "West," the developed capitalist countries. This shift is essential, for though we may not be Europeans, we are no doubt, as Alejandro Lipschutz has put it, "Europoids."

But we have another important heritage, which I would venture to call intermediate—neither indigenous, nor in the strict sense "Western," but rather, as I have suggested elsewhere, "Paleo-Western": our Iberian heritage. In any attempt, however modest, to specify the roots of our culture, we cannot gloss over our relationship to our Iberian background. My intention here is to present some general ideas on this relationship, emphasizing the evident poles: Spain and Spanish America.

It is obvious that a considerable part of our culture derives from a Spanish source. Although to speak of a "source" implies a metaphor and although the Spanish presence in the subsequent elaboration of our culture should not be exaggerated, neither should it be minimized; nor, indeed, should we attempt to obliterate it with the stroke of a pen. We received much more than a language from Spain; nevertheless, the peculiar form of that reception is revealed even in language. Ramón Menéndez Pidal, discussing the unity of the language, observed:

There are, we might say, two kinds of learned Spanish, just as there are two kinds of English, one European and the other American, which, in essence, are differentiated from one another by certain peculiarities of pronunciation.[1]

This visible (or, better still, audible) differentiation, which might also be called an enrichment, fortunately does not also entail the risk of linguistic fragmentation, as occurred with Latin after the fall of the Roman Empire, and as Andrés Bello and Rufino José Cuervo* feared (and fought) in the nineteenth century, because "the nations into which the Spanish Empire was divided are in closer communication today than when they constituted a single state."[2] While permitting variation and enrichment on both sides, the unity of our language has properly been preserved, thus guaranteeing fruitful communication and the survival of a homogeneous link to the rest of the world.

Beyond language, the situation is, of course, much more complex. Spanish Americans like to say about Spaniards that we do not descend from those who stayed but rather from those who came, whose offspring had already ceased to be Spaniards and were becoming first Creoles and, later on, after intermixing with other ethnic groups, Latin Americans. The logic of this distinction is clear: over a century and a half ago, Spanish America began its political break from the battered and decadent Spanish Empire, which was destined to lose its remaining American possessions, including Cuba in 1898. Moreover, the first definition of Spanish America was made in counterpoint to Spain, and it necessarily implied emphasizing our differences. It was, we are aware, a complex differentiation, one in which the urgency of pointing out what distinguished us from the old metropolis, unaccompanied by truly original solutions, contributed to the seduction of many by the lure of new and aggressive metropolises—as if changing masters, as Martí warned, were the same as being free.

The acceptance of proposals to "Westernize," which fascinated certain Spanish-American groups intent on modernization, was facilitated by the Spain's lamentable situation and the iniquitous exploitation it imposed on the territories where new nations were arising. But a contributing factor was that, beginning in the sixteenth century, Spain and its culture had been branded by an unrelenting anti-Spanish campaign that has come to be known as the Black Legend. It is worth pausing to consider this legend, uncritical acceptance of which, as we shall see, has had generally negative consequences, especially for ourselves.

---

* Andrés Bello (1781–1864). The great Venezuelan-Chilean educator, linguist, and grammarian is considered the founder of Latin-American language studies. The Colombian scholar, Rufino José Cuervo (1844–1911), was Bello's successor. A linguist, grammarian, and lexicographer, he was the founder of Latin-American philology. — Trans.

The Rationale of the Black Legend

To all appearances, the Black Legend originated in the justifiably shared rejection of the monstrous crimes committed on this continent by the Spanish conquerors. But a minimal respect for historical veracity indicates that this is simply false. The crimes were committed, and, yes, they were monstrous. But seen from the perspective of later centuries, they were no more monstrous than those committed by the metropolises that enthusiastically took Spain's place in this fearsome enterprise and sowed death and desolation on every continent. If anything distinguishes the Spanish conquest from the depredations of Holland, France, England, Germany, Belgium, and the United States, to mention a few illustrious Western nations, it is not the magnitude of the crimes, in which they are all worthy rivals, but rather the magnitude of the scruples. The conquests carried out by these countries were not lacking in death and destruction; what they did lack were men like Bartolomé de las Casas and internal debates on the legitimacy of conquest such as the ones inspired by the Dominicans, which shook the Spanish Empire in the sixteenth century. This does not mean that such men, always in the minority, succeeded in imposing their views, but they were able to argue their case before the highest authorities, and they were listened too and, to a certain extent, taken seriously. The French scholar Pierre Vilar, who has written on Spanish history with vast knowledge and a correct perspective, can argue:

> It is an honour for a colonial power to have had a Las Casas, and not to have exiled or disgraced him. In mid-century the School of Salamanca, with Melchor Cano, Domingo de Soto, and Francisco de Vitoria, lifted the discussion from the humanitarian to the juridical plane of "human rights," . . . It is imperative to distinguish between practice, no more brutal than any other type of colonization, and theory, with laws of the most noble intent (often absent in more recent colonial enterprise).[3]

It is also useful to note what scholars like Fernando Ortiz, Alejandro Lipschütz, and Laurette Séjourné, who have taken a clear stance against colonialism and in defense of the indigenous communities massacred by the Spanish Empire and those that came later, have had to say about the Black Legend. For Fernando Ortiz, "The conquest of the New World surely was extremely cruel," but "it was not so black or so legendary" given that:

> the blackness of its very human inhumanity was not exclusive to Spain or any darker than the other instances of genocide and subjugation by fire and blood and the most refined techniques when the uncontrolled desire for power and wealth darken peoples' conscience, even though they hide it with protestations about ideological fatalism, manifest destiny, natural predestination or service to God.[4]

Alejandro Lipschutz, for his part, maintains that

the Black Legend is *naive;* even worse, it is *malicious propaganda.*
Naive, because the conquistadors and the early colonists are no example
of the Spanish people's morals; malicious propaganda, because
seigneurial societies have carried out *all* their conquests in a similarly
fearful way and still do.[5]

Moreover, he argues that

[b]y the same logic, we ought to concoct an anti-Portuguese,
anti-British, anti-French, anti-German, anti-Russian, and anti-Yankee
Black Legend. There is nothing in the terrible events that Las Casas
succinctly labeled "the destruction of the Indies," that was determined
by the fact that the conquerors and early colonizers of America were
Spaniards, or, if you prefer, that they belonged to the Spanish "race."
Everything is determined by the fact that they were instruments,
whether blind or sighted, of a domineering *seigneurial regime
transported to an alien, tribal world by means of conquest. . . .* In the
pogrom of the conquest, the inner nature of the seigneurial regime is
made manifest. If you like, an anti-Spanish, anti-Portuguese,
anti-British, etc., Black Legend is inappropriate; what is appropriate is
an *antiseigneurial* Black Legend. And there is an even more important
historical fact: the truth is that it is not a matter of an antiseigneurial
legend but rather of a genuine, thousand-year-old *seignieurial reality.*[6]

Finally, Laurette Séjourné admits:

We have also realized that systematic accusations against the Spaniards
play a pernicious role in this vast drama, because they locate the
occupation of America outside the broad canvas of which it is a part,
since colonization is all of Europe's mortal sin. . . . No other nation
would have done any better. . . . On the contrary, Spain distinguished
itself by a gesture of capital importance: heretofore, it has been the only
country where powerful voices were raised against the war of conquest.[7]

These observations help us understand the real reasons for the rise and dissemination of the anti-Spanish Black Legend, which does indeed "locate the occupation of America outside the broad canvas of which it is a part." It is essential, therefore, to reject that mislocation and to locate the occupation of our
continent within that "broad canvas." Then we can see plainly that "at bottom,
the conquest and colonization of America in the sixteenth century is part of the
rise and consolidation of capitalism."[8] Those crimes can therefore be imputed to
the "rise and consolidation of capitalism," not to this or that nation. And they
reveal

the deep hypocrisy and *barbarism* characteristic of *bourgeois civilization*
as such, standing naked before our eyes when, instead of seeing it at

home, where it is on its best behaviour, we see it in the Colonies, where it removes its mask.[9]

The Black Legend was created and disseminated precisely to hide this truth, that "capital, [comes into the world] dripping from head to foot, from every pore, with blood and dirt,"[10] and to throw the blame on *a single nation,* Spain, which in the sixteenth century was the most powerful on earth and whose place, therefore, others desired, and plotted to, and finally did, take.[11] It was the nascent bourgeoisie of other metropolises who created the Black Legend, not, of course, for the benefit of those peoples martyred by the Spanish conquest but rather to cover up their own rapacity.[12] The Black Legend was thus a handy ideological weapon in the interimperial struggle that accompanied the rise of capitalism and lasted for several centuries, although by the end of the seventeenth century that struggle for all practical purposes had been decided in favor of new metropolises like Holland, France, and England, the major propagators of the legend. Naturally, in this struggle there were (and are) contradictions and mutual recriminations among the bourgeoisies of the respective powers, but they took place against a background of common interests similar to that of today's transnationals. This allowed them to praise one another not as the bandits they were (and are) but as the shining representatives of civlization *as such.* For example, the interimperialist contradictions that led to World War I at the beginning of this century were accompanied by the emergence of new Black Legends, just as mendacious as the original ones and, sadly, reflecting crimes just as real. They were forged by the warring contingents, to the detriment of their temporary enemies in the division of the world; they were products not only of the respective bourgeoisies but also, shamefully, of the traitors of the Second International, the pseudo-socialists who have left such a lamentable heritage to the present. But such legends did not continue to prosper once the war ended (nor, despite the horrors of nazism, did the anti-German Black Legend prosper after the Second World War), save in an attenuated and haphazard form typical of the ridiculous extremes of bourgeois national chauvinism. They did not prosper because it could not be otherwise among accomplices to the same crimes, especially not after the rise and ever more powerful development of the socialist world made possible the ongoing process of decolonization and forced the "civilized" barbarians to hurriedly remake their common cause. To give a name to this common cause—the cause of world exploitation, genocide, pillage and horror—they dusted off the terms "Western" and "Western culture," according to them the very essence of human splendor. This White Legend of the "civilized" West is the reverse of the original, and it has no other purpose or value. When it is not used as a murder weapon, it is simply idle chatter.

The Two Spains?

The means by which Spanish reactionaries have endeavored to combat the Black Legend have been, as we might expect, utterly ineffective. Reading their laborious texts,[13] one occasionally feels tempted to subscribe to the legend, which would be a serious mistake. Incapacitated by the narrow perspective of their class interests, they are content (in addition to insulting other countries) simply to make lists of sterile glories and worthless instances of national grandeur, while denigrating truly admirable individuals and achievements in Spanish history and culture. A characteristic example is the unanimous and bitter hatred expressed by Spanish reactionaries for the extraordinary Bartolomé de las Casas, to whom, presently, we shall have occasion to return.

The dichotomy shows that these writers, though afflicted with antidialectical mummification, are not entirely unaware of the duality that is at the heart of every national culture, as Lenin explained it.[14] The problem is that, claiming for themselves the totality of the Spanish heritage and blinkered by an ultrareactionary and clerical view of that heritage, they attempt to expel from it much of what we would consider vital and alive in Spain, blindly defending, by the same token, all that seems dead, ossified, and negative.

The only valid method is to begin by *explicitly* calling into question that false totality that would force us to accept or reject "Spanishness" en bloc — an absurd option — and proclaiming the existence not of one but of *two* cultures: seigneurial culture (as Lipschutz has it), and popular culture, the culture of the oppressors and the culture of the oppressed. The latter is for us the one that is truly alive, and we defend its works. But on this basis we can also proceed to consider the former without rejecting it out of hand (paying attention to Leninist praxis as well as theory), assimilating critically everything in it that is of general value to humanity.[15]

Indeed, few countries have expressed the consciousness of this duality as vividly as has Spain. Because of its advanced position in the early stages of capitalism and European expansion and its subsequent decline and eventual marginalization from the development of the capitalist system (which it was in some measure responsible for engendering), the question of an external duality (Europe/Spain) as well as an internal one ("the two Spains") becomes a constant of Spanish thought and letters almost from the beginning of the decadence, in the early seventeenth century.[16] Suffice it to recall Larra's* striking epitaph in "Día de difuntos de 1836" [All Souls Day, 1836]: "Here lies half of Spain: it died of the

---

* Mariano José de Larra (1808–1837), a journalist and playwright, was Spain's most important Romantic writer. Tormented by Spain's political problems, he took his life at the age of twenty-eight. The article "All Souls Day, 1836" was, in effect, his epitaph. — Trans.

other half.'' We might also remember that the magnificent poet Antonio
Machado,* who in works like ''El mañana efímero'' [The Ephemeral Future]—
written in 1913, the same year Lenin wrote of the existence of two cultures—
distinguished between two different Spains:

> La España de charanga y pandereta,
> cerrado y sacristía,
> devota de Frascuelo y de María,
> de espíritu burlón y de alma quieta.
> . . . .
> Esa España inferior que ora y bosteza,
> vieja y tahúr, zaragatera y triste;
> esa España inferior que ora y embiste
> cuando se digna usar de la cabeza,
> . . . .
> la España del cincel y de la maza,
> con esa eterna juventud que se hace
> del pasado macizo de la raza.
> Una España implacable y redentora,
> España que alborea
> Con un hacha en la mano vengadora,
> España de la rabia y de la idea.

> [The Spain of cymbals and tambourines,
> convents and sacristies,
> devoted to Frascuelo and Mary,
> cynical in sprit, deal of soul.
> . . . .
> That inferior Spain which prays and yawns,
> an aged gambler, querulous and sad;
> that inferior Spain which prays and charges
> when it deigns to use its head,
> . . . .
> the Spain of chisel and hammer,
> eternal youth sculpted from the
> rock-like past of our race.
> An implacable, redeeming Spain,
> Spain at dawn
> armed with an avenger's ax,
> Spain armed with fury and an idea.]

---

* Antonio Machado (1875–1939). Spain's greatest modern poet and a defender of the Second Spanish
Republic, he died in exile in France at the conclusion of the 1936–1939 Civil War.—Trans.

Without denying the evident existence of a *single* Spanish history, which in turn is part of world history, any consideration of Spain that fails to take into account the internal existence of these two cultures and insists on speaking of Spain in the singular, whether to denigrate or praise it, can only be legendary.

Spain and the West

It is not surprising, given its origin, that the Black Legend should find a place among the diverse and permanently unacceptable forms of racism. We need only mention the sad case of the United States, where the words "Hispanic" or "Latino" as applied to Latin Americans—to Puerto Ricans and Chicanos in particular—carry a strong connotation of the disdain with which the apparently transparent citizens of that unhappy country habitually deal with persons "of color." It may be useful, as well, to recall a statement attributed in its classical form to Alexandre Dumas: "Africa begins at the Pyrenees." The sacrosanct West thus shows its repugnance toward *the other,* which is not itself, and finds the embodiment par excellence of this *other* in Africa, whose tortured present was *caused* by Western capitalism, which "underdeveloped" it in order to make its own growth possible.[17]

By taking offense at Dumas's statement, Spanish reactionary thought again makes a muddle of things. What it demonstrates is that it is as racist as those who would subscribe to such a notion: for in fact Spain's capital sin was the doctrine of "purity of blood." Reality is always much more lively and instructive than those who are quick to lash out against what they consider an offense to their honor would normally imagine. The real history of Spain, not the one composed of official texts filled with empty rhetoric, shows us the utter untruth of what the West thinks about itself. I refer to that singular myth according to which Reason was revealed to Greece, became an Empire in Rome, and assimilated a Religion that was destined, after sseveral centuries in hibernation, to reappear like an armed prophet in the works of the (post-barbarian) Westerners, who were to spend the next several centuries fulfilling the onerous mission of bringing the light of "civilization" to the rest of the planet. If any country permits us to unmask the genial fraud implicit in this "history" appropriated by the developed Western bourgeoisie, it is Spain—a fact that no doubt has contributed in no small measure to the denigration it has suffered at Western hands. I do not pretend to be an expert on the matter, but common knowledge is sufficient to begin to rectify this mendacious cultural autobiography.

Over and against the stupid simplification according to which "Eternal Spain" was occupied for several centuries by Arab infidels whom she eventually succeeded in expelling from the pensinsula, thus preserving the purity of the Christian faith and keeping the contagion of Muhammadan barbarism from Europe, a much richer truth can be registered: Christians, Moors, and Jews, all equally Spanish, lived side by side for more than seven centuries, mutually and fruitfully influencing each other, as Américo Castro has explained in his controversial book. In that process, "one could never . . . state that what was Spanish was either European or Eastern." Moreover,

> Pressed by the charge of Islam and by French ambitions, Castile cultivated the clever, energetic style of a fencer, a master of thrusts and parries. The pressure of living under the threat of the world's highest civilization from the ninth to the twelfth centuries lead Castile to delegate to the Moors and Jews under its rule those tasks involving the world of things, technical prowess and sustained thought.[18]

Almost at the same time that Castro's book was published, Menéndez Pidal wrote:

> Although Southern Spain, Al-Andalus, developed a version of Islam that was highly Hispanicized in its customs, art, and ideology, it remain cut off from Europe and tied to the Afro-Asian cultural orbit. Northern, European Spain, although unyielding in its Christianity, fell under the influence of the south at a time when Arab culture was far superior to Latin culture, and thus it fulfilled the high historical destiny of acting as a link between the two orbits, East and West.[19]

Spain, in other words, was the conduit through which the influence of Arab civilization—"the world's highest . . . from the ninth to the twelfth centuries"—and Arab culture—"far superior to Latin culture"—entered Europe and brought new life to the still pallid European cultural world. This influence made itself felt in its philosophy, its literature, its science, its technology, its agriculture, its customs, in Aquinas, and in Dante. As the Spanish priest Miguel Asín Palacios pointed out, "Our nation can justly claim for some of its Muslim thinkers no small measure of the glory that criticism the world over has showered on Dante Alighieri's immortal work"[20]

But Spain was not only the "link between Christendom and Islam," as Menéndez Pidal put it. Because of the breadth of the Islamic world, Spain's function as a bridge was even more important for Europe, which gained access to the achievements of Greece, Persia, and India that the Arabs had assimilated. Think of the short story or of mathematics: remember the zero, an Indian invention that entered Europe through Arab Spain; the arithmetic book written at the caliph's urging by the ninth-century Persian Al-Khuwarizmi, who gave his name to our numbers (*alguarismo* in old Spanish; *guarismo* in modern). José Luciano Franco notes, in addition:

> The primitive Iberians were Negroid . . . From the Capsian peoples of the Moghreb came the immigrants who populated Iberia many millennia prior to our era; and it is the primitive Iberians who, in their traditional

contact with the peoples of its own ethnic group who stayed in Africa, gave birth to a phenomenon of transculturation that continued for more than twenty centuries and culminated with the Arabs, the Berbers, and the Sephardic Jews.[21]

It follows that, of the Spaniards singled out "for their cultural and linguistic traits as Arabs or Muslims" who were expelled with the Sephardic Jews in 1492, many were "in fact, Africans, mainly Berbers and Blacks."[22]

If we take all this into account, then it is not only Africa that, fortunately, begins at the Pyrenees but Asia as well. Moreover, this fact, along with many others, explains Europe's cultural reawakening in the twilight of the Middle Ages. If we also take into account the fact that the so-called Greek miracle had solid Afro-Asian roots, as we now know, and that Christianity itself was a beautifully quarrelsome Asiatic sect whose scandalous egalitarianism took hold among the slaves of the Roman Empire—just as, in Engels's classic analogy, socialism later would take hold among the new slaves of European capitalism,[23] then it becomes clear to what extent the West's idea of itself as a new "chosen people" is as false as similar ideas have been throughout history. Alejo Carpentier* likes to evoke the sad fate of the Carib people, a proud and bellicose community that extended from the shores of the Orinoco to the sea to which it gave its name (and its bones, to the cry of "Only the Carib is human"). When it sought to expand into the islands of the great sea, it collided with the proud and bellicose Spaniards, whose crosses and swords proved to be just as fragile as the arrows, war cries, and aboriginal canoes of the people they conquered. The implacable march of full capitalist development pushed aside Spain and her history, despite its debts to Spain (including her philosophical, artistic, scientific, technological, and juridical legacy to Europe) and her role as the vanguard of Europe's penetration of the New World (which, through her bloody extraction of gold and silver, generated the "primitive accumulation" destined to pass into the greedy hands of those Genoese and German bankers fond of referring sarcastically to the arrogant Spanish nobelmen as "our Indians"). In spite of everything, Pierre Vilar reminds us that

> Velázquez's Spain was still, however, an influential nation; it was the inspiration for France's *grand siècle,* and Castilian around 1650 was everywhere the language of civilisation. On the Isle of Pheasants (in the tapestry of Versailles) the august distinction of the Castilian court outshines the tasteless display of Louis XIV and his following. It was to be a long time before the *nouveaux riches* of England, the Low Countries and France herself could bring themselves to pardon Spain.[24]

---

* Alejo Carpentier (1904–1980). Cuba's most important novelist, he was, in addition, an excellent essayist and musicologist. His work is amply available in English. — Trans.

They were to "pardon" Spain with the Black Legend.

If it is understandable that the legend continues to live on in the reactionary sectors of the West, those for whom racism, mystification, resentment and irrationality are essential, it may seem less understandable at first sight that the legend still has currency in sectors considered part of the Western Left, where one would expect a more reasoned judgment of history. That this is so, nevertheless, exemplifies the sort of paternalistic European leftist who, as Jacques Arnault remarks, "denounces colonialism, but his hair stands on end when he finds the same denunciation in the writings of a colonial."[25]

As a case in point, consider a classic representative of a certain Western Left, Jean-Paul Sartre, expounding on Spanish culture in a manner Alexandre Dumas might have recognized as his own. To a (loaded) question put him by the journal *Libre,* Sartre replies: "When I first went to Cuba, I remember that one of the Cubans' chief concerns was to resuscitate their old culture, which unfortunately is Spanish, to guard against the absorbing influence of the United States."[26] One might think that Sartre is referring to the *present* situation of Spanish culture, which is lamentable indeed; but no, he speaks explicitly of *"their old culture, which unfortunately is Spanish."* Why insist on the obvious oversights? The old culture could be the native American, or the African, or the Creole, but for Sartre it is the old *Spanish* culture that is "unfortunate." In the countries that have risen out of colonialism, the old culture, if we omit as Sartre does the extra-European component, can only be the culture of the respective colonizers. Why the devil would we be more fortunate if our culture were Dutch, as in the case of Surinam, or English, as in Jamaica; or French, as in Haiti? How have these countries been favored over us by their relation to a non-Spanish metropolitan culture? Although he may not be aware of this, Sartre is doing nothing more in such remarks than subscribing to the Black Legend. The most important and definitive thing is that those countries born of colonialism, Cuba among them, have not only our respective old cultures but a new, revolutionary culture that we are creating together as well.

Jean-Jacques Fol offers another minor example of this same phenomenon in his evaluation of Las Casas. "No doubt," he writes, "Bolívar called Las Casas 'the Apostle of America,' and Martí sang his praises. But does this really suffice? Should we not be more farsighted?" Seeing farther than Bolívar and Martí is quite a task. Here is the mouse that the mountain of Monsieur Fol's "long view" brings forth: "After all, Father Las Casas's defense of America was accomplished to the detriment of Africa, and the salvation of the Indians was made possible by the arrival of slaves brought from Africa."[27] If this gentleman's ignorance were not as great as his telescopic fatuity, he would have needed only to have looked at a few maps of America (like the ones in Manuel Galich's essay "El indio y el negro, ahora y antes" [Indians and Blacks, Then and Now] to learn that where the "salvation of the Indians" occurred (the Mesoamerican plateau, the Andean sierra, etc.) are precisely the regions into which African slaves were *not* brought.[28] Rather, they were brought to work on the plantations of the coastal lowlands where the Indian *had already been exterminated*. But above all, Fol should have known that such a calumny against Las Casas, one of the noblest figures in human history, represents a base and reactionary canard. As Fernando Ortiz wrote back in 1938,

> Against Las Casas there was a dual desire, first, to erase from living memory the name of the man who criticized the barbarism of the conquest and destruction of the West Indies and, at the same time, when his name inevitably was brought up, to denigrate him, attributing to him the initiative for the slave trade . . . This was the outrageous calumny that the defenders of Spanish colonialism and slavery hurled at him.[29]

Ortiz would return to this question several times (as would such excellent and responsible scholars as Silvio Zavala and Juan Comas), especially in a definitive study, "La 'leyenda negra' contra Fray Bartolomé" [The 'Black Legend' against Father Bartolomé].[30] It is true that in the course of his dramatic and exemplary evolution, in which there was no lack of self-criticism, Las Casas, as was normal at that time among the Spaniards who had come to America, possessed detachments of commandeered Indian laborers (*encomiendas*) — before he became an impassioned defender of the Indians. And like everyone else at the time, including Thomas More in his projected *Utopia* of 1516, he believed slavery (both black and white, with no racial distinction) to be natural — before he commited himself to the impassioned defense of the blacks. But only a malicious, unthinking ignoramus would accuse Las Casas of being an *encomendero,* or a slaver, or of being anti-Indian or anti-black. Las Casas was not born Las Casas: like everyone else, he became who he was, although very few people achieved as much as he did. With full knowledge of the great Dominican's work and with the authority that his formidable scholarship on Cuba's African heritage confers upon him, Fernando Ortiz concluded his essay on Las Casas with these words:

> If Las Casas can be called "the Apostle of the Indians," he was also "the Apostle of the Blacks." History challenges his enemies to show texts in support of black slaves, against their capture in Africa and their transportation across the seas, their exploitation in America and their cruel treatment everwhere, that predate, and are more vivid and conclusive than, the writings of the great Spaniard, Bartolomé de las Casas.[31]

To this challenge, of course, Las Casas's detractors have as yet made no reply, which has not prevented them from spreading the nonsense that Monsieur Fol parrots, thus fueling the howling ultrareactionaries and helping to prolong the Black Legend against Father Bartolomé.[32]

Spain's Decadence

A point that I neither can nor wish to gloss over is the hoary cliché of Spain's decadence. That decadence is an incontrovertible fact but one that has nothing to do with supposed defects immanent to "Spanishness." The decline of an empire, which Spain would be the first modern nation to experience, had happened before and there would be other instances, such as Portugal, Holland, France, and even England—"the Queen of the Seas" back in our childhood, today a provincial lady more closely resembling Agatha Christie's Miss Marple. As each old empire declined, the new imperial power, the Yankee Empire, rushed helpfully in and, by hook or by crook, tried to inherit the former colonies. It wrested Puerto Rico and the Philippines from Spain; from France and Portugal it tried to inherit Indochina and Angola. As we know, the people of those countries have something else in mind.

The reasons for Spain's decline are well known, although some of them are still debated.[33] A series of disasters, such as the expulsion of the Jews and Moriscos and the crushing of the *comuneros* at Villalar by Charles V,* stifled the growth of the bourgeoisie and led to the recrudescence of feudalism that Ferdinand and Isabella had endeavored to check. The arrival of fabulous amounts of American treasure, in the absence of groups able to turn it into capital, sealed this regression. Pierre Vilar explains:

> The triumph of the *cristiano viejo* implied a certain contempt for money-making, even for the production of goods, and a certain attraction to the caste system. In mid-sixteenth century, the guilds began to oblige their members to prove their *limpieza de sangre*—a poor apprenticeship for entry into the capitalist age. . . . For some, the "Indian gold" served in itself to ensure Spanish hegemony—for others it is the root cause of Spanish decadence. . . . The profits were not "invested" in the capitalist sense of the term, and the fortunate emigrants dreamed of buying land, of building "castles" and of amassing treasure. The drama and the *Quixote* record this attitude in the peasant and the moble. . . . Recent pronouncements make a virtue out of Spain's incompatibility with capitalism, but this has condemned the country to inefficiency.[34]

This defeat of the bourgeoisie, this persistence of feudal structures, marked

---

* Charles V (1500–1558) was the first Spanish Hapsburg. Shortly after assuming the Spanish throne in 1517, he provoked an armed rebellion of the Castilian cities, the *comunidades*. The rebels, or *comuneros*, were crushed by the royal armies at Villalar in 1521. —Trans.

Spain's future. The survival of an archaic ideology embodied in an obscurantist Catholicism set bourgeois modernization against the straitjacket of the Counter-Reformation, causing the retardation (and even loss) of the scientific knowledge that was indispensable for the bourgeoisie (though not for feudal society).[35] In spite of efforts at reform in the eighteenth century, the outlook was grim at the beginning of the nineteenth, and Latin Americans could not fail to resent it bitterly. Upon returning from his journey to Spain in 1846, Sarmiento[*] would write with his habitual rudeness; "[At present] you [Spaniards] have no authors, no writers, no men of learning, no economists, no politicians, no historians, nor anything of the sort"; and in 1890, writing about the poet Sellés, Martí would state, "The Spanish-speaking peoples get nothing from Spain but rehashes." This is not necessarily a concession to the Black Legend but rather fidelity to the sad facts. The best Spaniards, from Larra to Costa,[†] said exactly the same thing. This is how a modern historian, Tuñón de Lara, describes the Spain from which Spanish America broke away:

> Spain was, at the beginning of the nineteenth century, a country that lived within the bounds of what has been called the *ancien régime*, that is, an overwhelmingly agrarian country dominated by large holding and seigneurial ownership, where the nobility and the church held most of the sources of wealth. . . . The vestiges of feudalism were so marked that, in many instances, ownership of land included the power of life and death over the villagers and peasants living on it.[36]

And, according to Roberto Mesa, "Nineteenth-century Spain is one great museum piece, the executor of the empire's last will and testament." What is more, given the annulment of the relative revival experienced between 1898 and the Civil War, Franco's Spain, "beyond all timelessness, fashionable technocracy, and the consumer society, is an immense grotesquerie [*esperpento*] that ranges from Goya's etchings to Valle-Inclán's[‡] bemedaled military men."[37]

This awful historical situation, this structural backwardness of a European country that never underwent a bourgeois revolution and remained overwhelmed by feudal remnants, explains the generally low level of its theoretical disputes, a fact that Cajal[§] alluded to. Beginning in the period when decadence is there for

---

[*] Domingo Faustino Sarmiento (1811–1888), Argentine writer, politician, and historian, author of *Facundo o civilización y barbarie* [Facundo: civilization or barbarism] (1945). He was president of Argentina from 1868 to 1874. — Trans.

[†] Joaquín Costa (1844–1911), Spanish scholar, educator, and political reformer, he argued vigorously for the Europeanization of Spain. — Trans.

[‡] Ramón María del Valle-Inclán (1866–1936). A bohemian novelist and playwright and Spain's most inspired modernist, he pitilessly satirized official Spain in his *esperpentos*, or grotesqueries. — Trans.

[§] Santiago Ramón y Cajal (1852–1934). A Spanish biologist, he was awarded a Nobel Prize in 1906 for his research on the human nervous system. — Trans.

all to see, many of her best thinkers became entangled in endless squabbles over the need to Europeanize Spain.[38] This, naturally, meant different things in different circumstances and generally lead to confused propositions, even in men as energetic and clear-minded as Costa. Consider, for example, the contradictory Unamuno,[*] who in *En torno al casticismo* [Regarding Spanishness] (1895) subscribed to Costa's quite reasonable thesis only to go to the other extreme, seeing some things clearly but irrationally closing himself off to others; or think of the Westerized Ortega,[†] a classic case of what Machado called "the tragic frivolity of our reactionaries"; or consider those who, at present, believe that a Spain yoked to the interests of the transnationals will be modernized. Plainly, Spain is in urgent need of modernization, but it will not be achieved through "Europeanization" or "Westernization." The latter, as Spanish America showed, can lead only to neocolonialism. Real modernization will come from profound structural change, with the revolution for which Costa cried out in anguish. But it will not be the bourgeois democratic revolution that he championed. It will move forward toward the socialist revolution prefigured in the Republic of 1936–39, which will turn Spain not into a Western but rather a post-Western country, just as in Russia in 1917 and Cuba in 1959. There is no Western (that is, developed capitalist) future for Spain. Today it is a paleo-Western country; in the future—soon, we hope—it will be a post-Western one.

Our Spain

This economically underdeveloped and, until recently, politically shackled Spain is a country that we Spanish Americans can only consider our sister: it is a country like ours. Its tormented past is also, in a way, ours; its sad present is similar to that of many of our countries (especially now that fascism is attempting to expand on our continent). Its future is very much our concern. With great pain, we see the descendants of harmonious Indo-American and African societies doing the hardest jobs in today's capitalist world. The destiny of the poor descendants of Spain's ruinous grandeur is scarcely different: those who do not languish in their own country are servants in France, miners in Belgium, unskilled workers in West Germany. This too gives us pain.

Fortunately, our hope of eventually seeing a revolutionary and victorious Spain is not based on mere sentimental illusions. Marx pointed out at the middle

---

[*] Miguel de Unamuno (1864–1936). A Spanish writer, poet, philosopher, and educator, he was considered the moral voice of early twentieth-century Spain. Many of his more important essays have been translated into English. — Trans.

[†] José Ortega y Gasset (1883–1955). The most influential Spanish philosopher of the twentieth century, he was a Nietzschean elitist who, in 1923, founded a monthly journal, the *Revista de Occidente* [Occidental Review]. — Trans.

of the nineteenth century that "Napoleon, who, like all his contemporaries, considered Spain a lifeless corpse, was given a deadly surprise on discovering that, although the Spanish state was dead, Spanish society was everywhere full of life and bursting with the force of resistance."[39] Forty years ago this fact was proven again: the glow of that example, which illuminated my childhood, has not been extinguished. Savagely attacked by the Fascist blitzkrieg that was later to cut through Europe like a knife through butter only to come to ruin against the magnificent Soviet people, Spain showed for three unforgettable years, from 1936 to 1939, how much it was still "full of life and bursting with the force of resistance." It is indicative of our solidarity with Spain that the best Spanish-American poets went to the peninsula in those years and wrote some of their finest poems in homage to the Spanish people's resistance: "Children of the world: / mother Spain is shouldering its womb," wrote impassioned César Vallejo. And there too, a symbol of our common dentiny, rests the generous Pablo de la Torriente Brau, "the sun of Spain in his face / and Cuba's in his bones," as his brother, Miguel Hernández would write. *

Is it really necessary to insist on the intimacy we now feel and always will feel for this other Spain, the Spain where Las Casa and the great Dominicans of the sixteenth century, "the most brilliant moment of hispanic anticolonialist thought,"[40] nobly defended the first Americans; the Spain of thinkers (even though many of them were forced to work outside Spain) like Vives and the Erasmists,[41] of Servet, Huarte, Suárez, Sánchez, Feijoo, Cadalso, Jovellanos, Blanco-White — and, for that matter, after the Independence of nearly all of Spanish America, Larra, Pi y Margall, the Krausists,[42] Costa, Pablo Iglesias, Cajal, some of the Generation of 1898[43] and above all Antonio Machado; the Spain whose people, in a dramatic undertaking, engendered the rebellious descendants of our America; the Spain of the *comuneros*, the guerrillas who fought Napoleon, the *cortes* of Cadiz, Riego and the Institución Libre de Enseñanza; the Spain of workers, peasants, and thinkers; the Spain that fought magnificently for all of humankind from 1936 to 1939 and lost once again? With the eyes of this Spain we can look upon the members of an extraordinary and complex family: the art of Arab Spain, the *Poem of the Cid,* Don Juan Manuel, the Archpriest of Hita, the *Celestina,* the medieval ballads and the picaresque novel, Garcilaso, Fray Luis, Ercilla, Saint Theresa, Saint John of the Cross, Góngora, Cervantes, Balbuena, Quevedo, Lope, Tirso, Ruiz de Alarcón, Calderón, Saavedra Fajardo, Gracián, El Greco, Velázquez, Moratín, Goya, Quintana, Espronceda, Bécquer,

---

* César Vallejo (1892–1938), the Peruvian poet, wrote the finest poetry to come out of the Spanish Civil War, his posthumous *España, aparta de mí este cáliz* (1939) *(Spain, Take This Cup from Me,* trans. Clayton Eshleman and José Rubia Barcia [New York, 1974]). The Cuban poet, Pablo de la Torriente Brau, gave his life in 1936 fighting for the Spanish Republic. He was memorialized by a great Spanish poet, Miguel Hernández (1910–1942), who, in turn, was imprisoned by Franco at the conclusion of the Civil War in 1939 and died in jail three years later. — Trans.

Rosalía de Castro, Valera, Galdós, *Clarín,* Unamuno, Baroja, Valle-Inclán, *Azorín,* Antonio Machado, Juan Ramón, Miró, Picasso, Gómez de la Serna, Manuel de Falla, León Felipe, Moreno Villa, Lorca, Alberti, Buñuel, Miguel Hernández . . . *

Is there any earthly reason why those infected with the Black Legend should presume to tell us that the error and horrors of Spanish reaction require us to forget what—in a parallel line—is also our heritage, should presume to make us ashamed of it? What sense does it make to pronounce the whole of a country's culture worthless because of the atrocities that certain sectors of that country once committed? Do we not admire Shakespeare, Shaw and Virginia Woolf in spite of the British Empire? Whitman, Twain, and Hemingway in spite of Yankee imperialism? Rebelais, Rimbaud, and Malraux in spite of French colonialism? Pushkin, Tolstoy, and Dostoyevsky in spite of the Czars? Goethe, Heine, and Brecht in spite of nazism? Dante, Leopardi or Pavese in spite of Fascism.[44] And even Kipling, Claudel, and Pound in spite of Kipling, Claudel, and Pound? The truth of the matter is that we are proud that what is Spanish is also ours; to do without it would not enrich us, it would leave us lamentably impoverished.

The exceptional case of José Martí suffices to demonstrate how the best of Spain's cultural heritage, mixed in with others, was transfigured in an American oeuvre. As Noël Salomon has pointed out, it is evident no one else in our America could create a vision of our culture's authenticity as encompassing and coherent; no one else could create an oeuvre as true to our aboriginal roots, as respectful of them and as loving, and as universally valid. No one was less likely to be blinded by the false and bloody light of an empire whose last chains he helped decisively to remove from our America. And yet, could a well-read reader fail to see that his modern, stylistically advanced, original, forward-looking work has its only artistic equivalent in the greatest writers of the Spanish Golden Age, writers whose work he knew and assimilated like no one else. Thus, Juan Marinello could speak of "José Martí's literary Spanishness."[45] Martí himself, referring to Quevedo, noted that "he plunged so far into the depths of the future that today we speak his language."

It was Martí who in *La edad de oro* [The Golden Age] taught the children of his America to love and respect Las Casas, who was Spanish ("as were his father and his mother"), to not confuse him with "those murdering conquistadors who must have come from hell—rather than Spain," who in his later years confessed:

> Para Aragón, En España,
> Tengo yo en mi corazón
> Un lugar todo Aragón:

---

* The interested reader is advised to consult P. E. Russell, ed., *A Companion to Spanish Studies* (London, 1974), and Philip Ward, ed., *The Oxford Companion to Spanish Literature* (Oxford, 1978).—Trans.

Franco fiero fiel, sin saña

· · · · · · · · · · · · · · · ·

Estimo a quien de un revés
Echa por tierra a un tirano:
Lo estimo si es un cubano;
Lo estimo si aragonés.

[For Spain's Aragon
There's a place in my heart
That's all Aragon:
Frank, fierce, faithful, free of hate

· ·

I respect a man who
slaps a tyrant to the ground:
I respect him if he's Cuban;
I respect him if he's Aragonese].

It was he who, while making ready for Cuba's War of Independence, was able to distinguish between "the Spaniard who stores his treasure, which is his only country, back in Santander or Barcelona," and "the simple, open Spaniard who loves liberty just as we do, whose country is justice," the "good, liberal Spaniard . . . my Valencian father, my montañés bondsman," and exclaimed, "Let someone else attack these Spaniards: I will defend them all my life." This man gave us a lasting lesson on the nature of the relation between Spain and America.

Following in Martí's footsteps and adding some of their own are Nicolás Guillén, author of the "The Surname," the extraordinary and exemplary poem in which he evokes his "two grandfathers" (one African, the other Spanish); and Mirta Aguirre, who brought a superb Marxist perspective to the study of Cervantes, showing how our revolutionary scholars should study our enormous Spanish cultural heritage.[46] And need we recall that when the legendary but utterly real hero of our America, Che Guevara, left Cuba to fight "in other lands," he wrote that he felt "Rocinante's ribs" under his heels? Frankly, and finally, I think Federico de Onís was right when he wrote:

We may assume that, someday, everything Spain established in America will disappear, just like the political structure of its colonial organization and other things belonging to the past—which are gone from Spain, as well—but the seed that those Spaniards who had the will to be Americans planted, which doubtless was the deepest expressions of the Spanish people, which possessed the greatest strength of unity, universality, and liberty, which was best suited to changing and adapting to a new reality, that seed will survive whatever changes may take place on a continent whose destiny is forever to search for something greater.[47]

—1976

Some Theoretical Problems of
Spanish American Literature

A Call to Action

In recent years, as Spanish-American literature has gained more widespread recognition and an international audience, the incongruity of approaching it with intellectual tools derived from other literatures has become increasingly apparent. Here a complex process of liberation—whose zenith is, for the time being, the Cuban Revolution—is paralleled by a complex literature whose best works express our problems and affirm our own values, critically assimilating diverse traditions and thereby contributing to our decolonization. This literature however, is itself still begging to be studied from a decolonized vantage point; usually it is presented as a mere projection of metropolitan culture—as something very different from what it actually is—often through an arbitrary system of values that places its formal experiments at the forefront and obscures its true functions, with varying ideological (and frequently diversionary) motives and consequences.

A scholar from the German Democratic Republic, Kurt Schnelle, takes this approach:

The Latin-American countries can be proud of their literary

Although these notes refer basically to Spanish-American literature, it is obvious that not a few of its observations could be applied equally to other literatures of our America: those of Brazil and the Francophone and Anglophone Antilles. In fact, some of the authors cited speak of *Latin-American* questions.

masterworks, which deserve to take their rightful place in world literature. . . . But Europocentrism did its best to accelerate the distantiation of literary themes and traditions from history and their approximation to play. Traditional literary concepts carried like a disease from the time of Goethe and other "classical" German poets have tenaciously held their ground. And so has the application to new literary phenomena of critical ideas derived from the classical bourgeois novel, with all the errors that implies, as we can see in the case of Lukács. In other words, Lukács presupposes an elective affinity between the bourgeoisie and the proletariat and thus denigrates and falsifies all of proletarian literature from Mayakovski to Brecht.[1]

And after mentioning the "the rather ridiculous notion that dialectical materialist methodology belongs to the past and that only a structuralist outlook can lead us to a scientific clarification of the literary phenomenon," Schnelle concludes:

Latin-American literary science, which could have given the rest of the world knowledge of the new literary phenomena of the continent, was held back in its presentation of recent literary production by the fact that in Europe there were "classics" to which, at first glance, the great works of the Latin American novel could not be compared.[2]

The Uruguayan writer Mario Benedetti is even more drastic in the questions he asks:

Should Latin-American literature at the height of its development submit to the canons of a formidably developed literature [that of Western Europe] that, nonetheless, is in a period of crisis?. . . . Should structuralist criticism be the unquestionable dictum of *our* letters? Or, on the contrary, should we, side by side with our poets and narrators, also create our own critical outlook, our own approach to research, put our own stamp on critical judgments stemming from our own conditions, our needs, our interests?

I am not proposing [Benedetti states further on] that, in the furtherance of our own critical values, we turn our backs to European views and contributions. . . . In Latin America we know that our region *is not* the world; therefore it would be stupid and suicidal to deny all that we have learned and have yet to learn from European culture. But this learning process, no matter how important it may be, cannot substitute for a pathway to our own convictions, our own set of values, our own sense of direction. We are in the vanguard in several areas, but in the area of critical judgment we still are beholden to Europe.[3]

These views stem from the unavoidable exigencies of our historical process. Thus it is not surprising to find a similar call to action in ongoing discussions across the continent and even worldwide. It is present in some of my own writing, as well,[4] and I would like to complement that work with the following notes.

General, Colonial, Racist

We already know that when Latin-American theoreticians absolutize certain European models, they often believe they have arrived at "general" conclusions, which they endeavor in some instances to exemplify with Latin American literary works. This method, rather than validating the "general" nature of their theory, usually reveals their colonial status. To such misguided efforts that I have mentioned in previously works can now be added *Teoría literaria general* [General Literary Theory] by the Argentinean scholar David Maldavsy.[5] In it, apart from a variety of speculative ideas, certain criteria derived from structuralism and psychoanalysis are applied eclectically to writers of our area.

There are, of course, writers who are aware of the arbitrariness of that method. In *La creación poética* [Poetic Creation] the Chilean neo-Thomist José Miguel Ibáñez hastens to explain that it is "the observations of Goethe, Poe, and Benn, and, above all, those of Rilke, Valéry and Eliot" that have provided material for this theory of the poem"[6] and although he mentions "the 'Latin Americanization' of the examples," he confesses a bit cavalierly in the definitive version of his book that "it is still a colonizer—for it applies a European treatment to Latin-American material." This, for him,

> without giving offense to anyone, is the basis of the sole possibility, for
> the time being, of taking a nonimpressionistic approach to our poets.
> . . . If present-day Latin-American poetry provides material rich enough
> to create and exemplify a philosophy of poetry, the time of
> self-knowledge soon may be at hand when we will be able to think
> philosophically without the "incurable historical hybridization," in
> Vallejo's words, that is this book's inevitable failing.[7]

Indeed—such is the inevitable failing of a book whose author not only is unaware that the "time of self-knowledge" came long ago to Latin America. Faithful to the deliriously irrational words of Rilke with which he begins his book, as a sort of exergue ("Works of art are infinitely alone, and there is nothing that is less able to grasp them than criticism"), he performs a task that at very minimum is useless, especially for ourselves.

But if in these kinds of books the very authors—conscious of their failings or at least of their limitations—speak critically of themselves as "colonizers" or refer to their supposed "general" validity (a term that often is nothing but a meliorative synonym of "colonizer"), there are, on the other hand, books that aspire to absolute fidelity to the peculiarities of our literature of our world, but are

inept in other ways. Perhaps the most common way — surely the archetypal one —
is an urge to ontologize, of which the German-Argentinean Rudolf Grossmann
gives us a number of examples in his *Historia y problemas de la literatura latinoamericana* [History and Problems of Latin-American Literature]. It is not my
intention to comment on this book's more than 750 pages, which lack neither for
useful contributions nor for a variety of errors; however, I must point out where
the belief in the spiritual fixity of a no less fixed "race" can lead. When speaking
of "the ethnic elements of the Latin American synthesis," the author can write
without blinking that

> the arrival of blacks as a replacement for the not very resistant Indians
> means not only cheap, reliable labor in the torrid tropical plains but a
> new emotional register as well: innocence and servility, extreme
> changeableness due to a lack of self-control and emotional stability; in
> contrast to the Indian, the prototype of monumental immutability.[8]

The nonsense deepens later on, when we read that wherever blacks are dominant,
the following characteristics "reign victorious":

— a sensuality, stronger even than in the mestizo or the Creole, born of
  a lack of self-control in their emotional life and bolstered by
  exuberant fantasy, a love of physical well-being and the verbally
  eloquent expression of same;
— a lack of reasoned political and economic thought, leading to discord
  and, at times, absurd rebellions: tyranny and cruelty go hand in hand
  with a spiritual weakness that can descend into servility;
— an exaggerated desire for notoriety — tending toward superficial
  dignity—and an inclination toward showy behavior;
— a fundamentally religious idea of things expressed in the primitively
  sensorial symbolism of paleo-religious fetishism or in a sort of
  primitive Christianity, which is typical of North American black
  spirituals as well;
— a stronger tendency than among Creoles to appropriate European
  cultural traditions. But whereas Creoles assimilate them when they do
  accept them, blacks usually settle for the naive adaptation of purely
  external forms, resulting in caricature.

After this, it is not surprising that, for the author, "what is truly 'evolu-
tionary,' the motor force behind the Latin-American literary synthesis" can be
found in "the modern human element of Western Europe and the United States
(46).

To these racist aberrations Grossmann adds historical aberrations, such as the
view that "in the Indian's passivity in the face of life's vicissitudes and his disdain for material goods, one can find the antidote to restlessness and greed. From
this vantage point, the Indian slowly emerges as the socialist antipode to capital-

ism and the representative of a new and more just social order''(62), et cetera. Although Grossman is right to reject ''the so-called immanent interpretation'' (28) in the study of our literature and occasionally is able to make valid observations, the very foundation of his outlook is irremediably harmed by the erroneous conception of history brutally manifest in his astounding racism—which of course, would be no more acceptable if instead of the peculiar characteristics that he attributes to one or another ''race,'' he were to propose a different distribution of traits. What is essential is that Grossmann locates ''races'' at the margins of history and replaces history itself with plainly inept ''biologically rooted'' characteristics of which Gobineau or Hitler would have approved. And when Grossmann does return to history, he sees it as a picturesque panoply from which, like a fiction writer, the scholar can choose and mix periods at will. Clearly, such puerile notions can hardly be helpful in working out the concepts that are proper to our literature, to our world.

Understanding Our World

The basic precondition for understanding our literature, as Mariátegui never tired of saying, is to be found outside literature: it is the understanding of our world, which in turn demands a thorough understanding of the larger world, of which we are part.[9] And that understanding can be achieved only with an adequate scientific tool, with dialectical and historical materialism, which, it bears repeating, is the opposite of a series of formulas, a mess of pottage to be applied without distinction to any and all reality.[10] On the contrary, as has been stated so many times—never, it seems, too many—Marxism is not a dogma but a guide to action, including of course the sort of action that involves theory. Theory is not a finished product, for the soul of Marxism, said Lenin, is ''the concrete analysis of concrete conditions.''

In our case, it will not do simply to apply criteria based on other realities (criteria that, at best, were born of the analysis of *different* conditions) or to turn our backs on history, cut ourselves off from other realities, and enumerate our own real or imagined characteristics with an eye toward proclaiming an absurd segregationist difference from everyone else. We must make plain our ''concrete conditions.''

Because he rejects both temptations and because he starts out from a reasoned view of history, the Brazilian critic Antônio Cândido, taking into account the specifically colonial nature of our origins and the ''underdevelopment'' that is its consequence—terms implying a determinate, necessary *relation*—reminds us that ''our continent is characterized by outside intervention'' and ''cultural dependency'' and that ''it is illusory to speak of the supression of contacts and influences.''[11] And he adds:

Is there a paradox in this? Indeed, the better a free, thinking man
understands the tragic reality of underdevelopment, the more he opens
himself to revolutionary inspiration, that is, the more he believes in the
need to reject the economic yoke of imperialism and to transform the
internal structures that feed the situation of underdevelopment.
Nonetheless, he looks more objectively at the problem of influences,
seeing them as a cultural and social tie. The paradox is more apparent
than real and it constitutes a sign of maturity impossible to attain in the
closed and oligarchic world of nationalist ideology. To such an extent is
this the case that the recognition of an inner linkage is associated early
on with the ability to innovate in the area of expression and to struggle
in the area of economic and political development.[12]

This, of course, leads us in the first place to pose questions about that
"broader culture" of which we are a "cultural variety." "Culture," we know, is
a word that has many meanings, and this is not the time to discuss its rich
diversity.[13] Let us simply recall that its most general meaning suggests all that
humankind adds to nature—including the ways that we have changed nature itself—and in another sense refers to the sum total of a national community's characteristics. And there is no doubt that although it exhibits appreciable differences
which signify "varieties," that sum total—or, better yet, that system—of social
sign systems constituting a culture—can and often does take in supranational
areas.[14] Such is the case of that "broader culture" of which Cândido speaks.
Nonetheless, a surprised observer might ask, "Isn't this merely that self-same
European culture whose arrogant claim of universality we are agreed in rejecting?" This is the time to recall that the acceptance of that "Europe" as a virtually homogeneous and timeless bloc—which we perpetuate by internalizing or
which we attempt, in a fit of anger, to impugn—already implies, whatever our
reaction may be, a colonized attitude. Just as it is fraudulent to identify "American" with "the United States" (as so often is the case *over there*), it is equally
fraudulent (as so often occurs, this time, over here) to identify "Europe" with a
handful of Western European countries with highly developed capitalist econo-
mies, forgetting that the real Europe is not only London and Paris but Sophia and
Bratislava as well, not to mention the obvious internal diversity of those same
countries, which have produced nazism and the Commune, Rhodes and Marx.
    Our maturity demands that we reject that simulacrum of "Europe" that passes
off certain local characteristics as universals and proclaim that the real Europe,
the one without quotation marks, just yesterday included highly developed capitalist countries and backward countries, colonizing and imperialist countries as
well as colonized countries, ascending bourgeoisies and declining bourgeoisies,
reactionary movements and workers' and peasants' struggles, colonialist and imperialist wars of pillage along with wars of national liberation, Italian fascism
and the Spanish Revolution, and today includes capitalist countries, developed as

well as underdeveloped — with great internal contradictions — and socialist countries. How are we to demand attention and respect for our specificities if we begin
by denying attention and respect for the specificities of others? So, the "broader
culture" to which Cândido refers *is not* simply identified with that of "Europe."
In any event, we would accept its identification with those countries of Europe,
America, Oceania and other areas to which "Europods," the term used on occasion by the Lithuanian-Chilean Marxist scholar Alejandro Lipschütz, might by
applicable.[15] And although, as Lenin postulated, we will not refuse to inherit
critically whatever may be positive in it, this means that *we would utterly refuse*
to identify that "culture" with the one that a restricted, colonialist, reactionary
sense, some people take to be "Western Culture." It is something far more vast,
geographically and historically speaking, and it implies a wide, rich and dynamic
world in which there are numerous affinities ("sympathies," Reyes would call
them) and differences. These last are obvious: suffice it to recall the plurality of
languages, to point up perhaps the most evident one. But with regard to affinities, it is illuminating to see the way the Hungarian scholar Miklos Szabolsci as-
sessed his literature in a meeting held in France in 1969:

> The problem of the explosion of language's outer shell is not posed in
> Hungary, because the language itself, particularly the spoken language,
> is undergoing constant change. . . . [T]he logical discourse that so
> constricts you [French] has not yet been created here. . . . A second, no
> doubt more important, preliminary observation: not in reference to
> nineteenth-century romanticism but rather on the basis of sociological
> research, literature in our culture taken as a whole, in people's general
> consciousness, is more important in Hungary than in France. For a long
> time we did not have great philosophers. In the eighteenth and
> nineteenth centuries, great ideas were not expressed in the form of
> theory (we had no Voltaire, no Marx, no Freud) but in the works of
> poets, especially lyric poets. Thus, not only is our cultural model more
> literary, but poetry occupies a privileged position. Still today, even in its
> most hermetic forms, ordinary people read quite a lot of it.
> Furthermore, this state of affairs is not exclusive to Hungary: it is to be
> found in Spain, Latin America, and some of the Eastern countries,
> including Russia. In other words, the model of French literature cannot
> be taken as an immutable model. Moreover, the role of certain literary
> tendencies and schools is a bit different in a country like ours from that
> in France or Germany, for example. French symbolism had an
> extraordinary impact in Romania, where it was a school of great poets
> but at the price of a transformation, an adaptation, a folklorization.
> Beginning in 1930, surrealism played an important role in
> Czechoslovakia, although it was wedded to another tradition in a
> synthesis that was quite distinct from the French model. Problems
> relating to the interplay of form, content, function, value have also

changed their appearance and their purpose. Since we have brought up the role of literary sociography—writing that is halfway between literature and document—I should indicate in closing that it is infinitely more important in Hungary than in other countries.[16]

Szabolsci shows his awareness of the similarities among "minor" Western literatures: they convergence notably in spite of differences born of dissimilar origins and languages and despite a lack of contact that in some cases has been enormous. These similarities are no accident: they are engendered by the rise of the respective countries as modern nations on the periphery of the most developed capitalist countries. The relations they have maintained with those developed countries, along with their own internal development, have contributed decisively to their present status.[17]

A good ten years ago when I wrote on Martí and pointed out the similarities in the economic and political conditions imposed upon the colonial and semicolonial countries of Asia, Africa, and Latin America—which, quite equivocally would be called the Third World—I called attention to the fact that

Latin America finds itself in a unique situation. Whereas the "Westerner" is a mere intruder in most of the colonies he has pillaged, in the New World he is in addition one, and not the least important, of the components that will give rise to the mestizo (not just the racial mestizo, of course). If "Western tradition" is not the New World's entire tradition, it is its tradition *as well*. Thus there is a more delicate counterpoint among Latin-American thinkers compared to those of other colonized areas.[18]

What I did not see clearly enough back then is that our "unique situation" was not quite so unique. Greater direct knowledge of the *other* Europe, of our America, and of Asia, and a closer study of certain facts and authors has shown me how similar some of Latin America's characteristics and problems are to those of Europe's periphery, where socialist revolutions were also to develop.

Furthermore, the structural similarities between the countries of Latin America and those of the *other* Europe had already been observed by Lenin himself in his preparatory notes for *Imperialism: The Highest Stage of Capitalism*.[19] These notes, which are of unquestionable interest despite their brevity, have scarcely received the attention they merit. The similarities themselves, however, also deserve further study.[20] It could be said that the language of recent years has already taken account of them. When someone speaks, in a revealing meaphor, of the balkanization of our America, does this not suggest a parallel between two areas of the planet that invites further study? We owe some of the scant material that we have found on this topic to the always sagacious Lipschutz, who pointed out the parallels between socioeconomic problems of the old Russian Empire and those of Latin America in our own time.[21]

Similarities between socioeconomic problems such as those suggested by Lenin and Lipschütz, on the one hand, and cultural parallels of the kind that suggest a more vast and enriched culture, on the other: there can be no better time to propose the development of comparative studies of our respective literatures, studies that surely would reveal singular aspects of both, as Szabolsci shows. Of course, this requires us to reject the curious limitation imposed by Ulrich Weisstein upon such studies when he declares that "the notion of influence ought to be considered the key concept of Comparative Literature."[22] To take this criterion literally, and apply it to our letters would produce a colonizing concept of comparative study and would explain the existence of those cheery pleonasms like "Alexandre Dumas in Havana" or "Shakespeare in Tegucigalpa." No, the key concepts of such studies (not discarding that of influence, but putting it to a different use) ought rather to draw attention to the structure and function of the literary works in question, even if we are unable to speak of influences between them.[23] Unfortunately, I do not believe that very much has been done along these lines. We can, however, see what is to be gained from this kind of work in the comparison done by the Soviet scholar Vera Kuteishchikova of Soviet and Mexican narrative in the early days of their respective revolutions,[24] or in the review in which the Romanian scholar Adrián Marino points to the similaries between Martí's criticism and that of Romanian critics of the same period:

Indeed between the ideas of José Martí, the great Cuban poet, critic and revolutionary of the late nineteenth century, and some essential problems of Romanian criticism (which was just beginning to take shape), we can find a commonality of stances, dilemmas, and solutions that are parallel and, on occasion, utterly identical. The explanation can be found in the general orientation of European, especially French, criticism, which was very influential at the turn of the century, as well as in the natural reaction of minds that were deeply concerned with the creation and consolidation of a criticism that simultaneously would be modern and national, criticism resulting from the rejection of all forms of spiritual "colonization" or pure and simple colonialism, as in the well-known case of José Martí.[25]

Nevertheless, the development of *this* comparativism is impeded not only by the aforementioned colonialist criteria but also by what we might call the pathetic bovarism of writers and scholars from these peripheral countries, which leads some Latin Americans as well as some of those other Europeans to imagine themselves as exiled metropolitans. For them a work produced in their immediate orbit, not to mention a work produced on the transatlantic periphery, merits their interest only when it has received the metropolis's approval, an approval that gives them the eyes with which to see it. These are the real outsiders, the hopelessly colonized, who seem not to understand that, with the rise of socialism, the capitalist countries are the ones standing outside the main line of history.

Demarcations

When posing specifically literary questions, the first, basic, problem is to elucidate what is and what is not literature. Alfonso Reyes saw that task as the "prolegomena to a literary theory," in the book that is still the Spanish-American classic on the subject: *El deslinde. Prolegómenos a una teoría literaria* [The Line of Demarcation: Prolegomena to a Literary Theory].[26] With extreme acuity and complex critical tools,[27] Reyes sets out to establish the limits between literature and other human products: history (the science of the real), mathematics, theology. But he realizes that before undertaking the arduous drawing of distinctions, we first must draw another line:

> Before confronting literature with nonliterature, we first must decant the liquid and separate out the silt. Our object will be to recognize the liquid as liquid and the silt as silt, but not so as to deny different mixtures their rights, much less their existence. To correctly distinguish in literature between what is pure, substantive agency and what is adjectival or ancillary, we shall study the ancillary function. [*D*, 29]

Just prior to this he had stated:

> Without a certain set of concerns, there is no literarature in a pure state, only literature applied to alien concerns, literature as a service or ancilla. In the first case—drama, novel, or poem—the object of expression is fulfilled in expression itself. In the second—history with rhetorical window dressing, science made easy, bonbon philosophy, a sermon, or a religious homily—literary expression serves as a vehicle for subjects and purposes that are not literary.[*D*,26]

And he adds: "If, then, there is in literature a substantive phase and an adjectival one, we may discard the latter in order to keep the former" (*D*, 30).

No doubt about it. For Reyes there is, on the one hand "literature in a pure state," "liquid," "pure or subtantive agency," "essence," which manifests itself in "drama, novel, or poem," where "the object of expression is fulfilled in expression itself"; and, on the other hand, there is "literature applied to alien concerns, literature as a service or ancilla," "silt," the different mixtures of which are considered an "adjectival or ancillary" agency worthy of Reyes's smiling irony: "history *with rhetorical window dressing*," "science *made easy*," "*bonbon* philosophy" (emphasis mine), where "literary expression serves as a vehicle for subjects and purposes which are not literary."

These notions, which Reyes derives from his phenomenological—or "pheno-menographic," as he preferred, to avoid confusion,—point of view,[28] link him to other, relatively recent demarcations, although Reyes's are usually much more minute and careful. The one that achieved perhaps the greatest notoriety was expounded by the then Russian Formalist Roman Jakobson in *New Russian Poetry: The First Sketch—Velimir Klebnikov,* a text with which Reyes does not seem to be familiar—not surprisingly, since it was written in Russian, published in Prague in 1921, and brought out in fragmentary form in French in 1973. In that piece is found Jakobson's oft-quoted (in second- or thirdhand versions) definition: "The object of the science of literature is not literature but literariity, which is to say, what makes a given work a literary work."[29]

Along with this observation of Jakobson's to which so many formalists and para-formalists would subscribe,[30] let us set aside two others:

1. "A scientific poetics is possible only if it renounces all acts of judgment: would it not be absurd for a linguist, in the practice of his profession, to judge the comparative merits of adverbs?" (*QP,* 12–13).[31]

2. "To make poets assume responsibility for ideas and feelings is as absurd as would be the behavior a medieval public if it beat the actor who played the role of Judas" (*QP,* 16).

A literary science that states its refusal to judge; a writer who is not responsible for the ideas and feelings expressed in his work: this emptiness is the counterpart of Jakobson's "literariity"—which despite its noisy pretense of modernity, is nothing but a tardy corollary of the nineteenth-century theory of "art for art's sake"—ingeniously defended by him in the following terms: "[U]ntil now, literary historians seemed rather like the policeman who, wanting to arrest someone, arbitrarily hauled in everyone in the house, along with a few passersby." *QP,* 15). Such a procedure, as we readers of mysteries well know, is grossly defective. But what Jakobson proposes is that the literary historian-policeman, upon entering the house, ought forthwith to arrest the butler. And this, as we readers of mystery novels also know, is no less ridiculous and false than the first procedure.

But if this position is unacceptable, Jurij Tynjanov,—another Russian Formalist—possibly the one who took things furthest—indicated three years later in 1924, in "The Literary Fact," apropos of the concept of "literature," that "all of its static and fixed definitions are liquidated by evolution. The definitions of literature built upon its 'essential' features are smashed against the *living literary fact.*"[32] And further: "Only at the level of evolution are we able to analyze the 'definition' of literature."(31). It is just this evolution that reveals to us not only that the "limits, its 'periphery' and its frontier zone" are unclear, but so is its very center; thus, what was the "center" can become marginal and vice versa.(27).

Three years after that essay, in 1927, Tynjanov complemented it with another one, "On Literary Evolution," where he points out the way in which

The very existence of a fact *as literary* depends on its . . . function. What in one epoch would be a literary fact would in another be a common matter of social communication, and vice versa . . . Thus the friendly letter of Derzavin is a social fact. The friendly letter of the Karamzin and Pushkin epoch is a literary fact. Thus one has the literariness of memoirs and diaries in one system and their extraliterariness in another.[33]

These ideas, which would be developed in Brecht's literary theory (and praxis)[34] and in the best work of the Prague Circle,[35] are undoubtedly fertile when we stand before a literature like that of Latin America.

From the outset, we must avoid the aprioristic attempt to *draw the lines of demarcation* of our literature: rather than *superimposing* the lines, we shall *ask questions* of our literature, of its concrete works.

In 1951, José Antonio Portuondo, in trying to bring into relief "the predominant characteristic of the Spanish-American novel," had already said:

The *dominant* characteristic in the Spanish-American novelistic tradition is not . . . the overwhelming presence of nature but rather social concern, the critical attitude its works make manifest, its *instrumental function* in the historical process of the respective nations. The novel for us has been a document of denunciation, a propaganda poster, a demand for attention to the gravest and most urgent social problems directed, as a spur to immediate action, toward the mass of readers.[36]

Nearly twenty years later, Portuondo would no longer limit that "*dominant characteristic*" to the novel and would write:

There is a *constant* in the Latin-American cultural process that is determined by the predominantly *instrumental* — Alfonso Reyes would say "ancillary" — character of literature, in the service, more often than not, of society. . . . From the outset, the verse and prose to which the Hispanic lands of the New World gave rise reveal an attitude toward their surroundings and attempt to influence them. There is no important writer or work that does not open up to America's social reality, and in even the most evasive of them there is an instant of apologetics or criticism of things and people.[37]

If the thesis of *functional instrumentality* as the dominant mode of Spanish-American literature is acceptable, as I believe it is, then we must examine Reyes's *line of demarcation,* according to which there is an essentially literary quality — literarity truly made manifest — in certain works that supposedly stand at the very center of literature, as opposed to hybrid works that stand necessarily at literature's margins, born where literarity is "mulattoed" by other functions.

But, as it happens, the main line of our literature is a mulatto, a hybrid, an "ancilla," whereas the purist, the strictly (and narrowly) "literary" one is marginal. And the reason for this is clear: given the dependent, precarious nature of our historical existence, it has fallen to literature to assume functions that in the metropolises have been segregated out of it. Thus, the colonized writers who reproduce or mechanically apply the structures and tasks of metropolitan literature to Latin America usually are not very effective and generally produce flawed or useless work, insignificant pastiches. Conversely those who do not reject the hybridity that the function of our literature demands are most often our really creative writers. Our literature confirms Tynjanov's criteria, verifying not only the invalidity of the aprioristic limits of literature but the way that what seemed (or was) central can become marginal and vice versa. Ignorance of these facts explains the incongruence of those who, apropos of Martí, Latin America's greatest writer (Reyes rightly called him "the supreme literary master,"[D, 213], ignoring, by the way, some of his own ideas on *lines of demarcation*), have deplored the "ancillary" nature of that great oeuvre, which, they argue, could not develop within the supposedly major genres. And so, because they accept alien categories, they are unaware that, just like the air for Kant's dove, the "ancillary" nature of our literature was not an obstacle but rather the condition of the concrete greatness of Martí's concrete work, the faithful and archetypal expression of the literature of our America.

Genres

We have not devoted enough attention to these facts, which force us to do some rethinking and, at the very outset, to admit the predominance in our letters of genres considered to be "ancillary": chronicles like the Inca Garcilaso's, speeches like those of Bolívar or Fidel; articles like Mariátegui's; memoirs like those of Pocaterra or many of the so-called novels of the Mexican Revolution;[38] diaries, not subjective elucubrations (Amiel, Gide) but rather Che Guevara's campaign diaries, "sociographic" forms like *Facundo* and many present-day testimonies. It is not an accident but a demonstrable fact that Martí did superb work in these and in similar genres—the epistolary, for instance. Other, supposedly more central—in our case, plainly marginal—genres pale by comparison, although to stick to the facts, we must make an exception of poetry—where, not incidentally, Martí was also outstanding.

Thirty years ago, the North American Marxist critic H. R. Hays pointed out that "it may be no exaggeration to state that in world literature, Spanish America's finest contribution is poetry."[39] We must add, however, that our poetry often is instrumental in its preferences and, in any event, is often strikingly different from that of the metropolises. Szabolsci, who pointed out that in our countries "poetry occupies a privileged position," also pointed out that symbolism in Romania "was a school of great poets, but at the price of a transformation, an adaptation, a folklorization." Cannot that "transformation," that "adaptation," that "folklorization," be found in our most creative and authentic poetry? It could very well be that the desire of many romantics to return to popular sources fully explains the existence of a poem such as *Martín Fierro*. But it should not be forgotten that this essential work of our poetry is so tremendously original that when it came out, although the more or less conventional Argentine writers of the day wrote the author celebrating his work, "it is doubtful," observed Pedro Henríquez Ureña with his habitual acuity, "that any of them considered it to be 'literature,' just as, about that very time, learned musicians in the United States would have thought that Stephen Foster's songs were excellent in their way, but not 'music,' that is, not the sort of things heard in concerts."[40] As for modernism, so "gleamingly imitative"[41] in its early phase, only those changes can explain how its maturity could lead to Rubén Darío's *Canto a la Argentina* [Song to Argentina], Leopoldo Lugones's *Poemas solariegos* [Manorial Poems], and the encounter with our realities that we find in Gabriela Mistral's *Tala* [Felling of Trees]: and the same can be said, taking into account the variants of each particular case, of our avant-garde literature, shaped by the deep mestizo voices of Vallejo and Guillén, or Pablo Neruda's *Canto general,* [General Canto], which recuperates and broadens Bello's project.

At times not only literary tendencies but even verse forms undergo a curious functional mutation in our countries. There can be few more exemplary cases than that of the *décima*. Arising in Spain in the second half of the sixteenth century in learned circles, as is evidenced by its complex architecture, it would nevertheless become the favorite verse form of a large part of Spanish-American popular poetry.[42] "It appears solely in the popular poetry of Spanish America," states Magis.[43] What makes it even more interesting is that in the Spanish Antilles, where the primacy of the *décima* began, the traditional form preferred by learned poets (although it never was very deeply rooted), was the *romance,* the favorite form of Spanish traditional poetry.[44] Carolina Poncet, the finest scholar of the *romance* in Cuba, has pointed this out repeatedly: "*Romances* have never become a popular literary genre in Cuba"; "the *romance* has always been an exotic plant here"; "where the *espinela* truly flowers is in genuinely popular Cuban poetry"; "the more popular a literary movement is or tries to be, the more important the *décima* becomes for it."[45] It would not be amiss to point out that most of *Martín Fierro* is written in the rather curious form of truncated *décimas*,[46] for the *décima* is the habitual form used by the *payadores* of the River Plate region, and the extraordinary Violeta Parra wrote her autobiography in *dé-*

cimas. Indeed, both works are superb examples of the fusion of learned and popular poetry in Spanish America.

I have spent some time—far less than I would have liked—in the *décima/romance*, learned/popular relation, because it is an excellent example of how only concrete historicity, rather than an a priori approach, can reveal the true characteristics and functions of a literary fact. A complex, learned form in Spain becomes popular in Spanish America, while we give the freest form developed by the Spanish people the stamp of learned poetry: this is just one instance of many similar mutations. Does not the simple, colloquial, metaphor-free tone of present-day Spanish-American poetry reveal its learned provenance, whereas—paradoxically, it would seem—popular poetry, especially when it relies on *décimas*, uses an intricate language filled with complicted metaphors that harks back to the baroque. But we have strayed from our subject—poetry's dominance in our literature, at least among the genres that are not obviously ancillary.

Upon returning to our subject, however, our first task will be to question this assertion of poetry's dominance, for if we were to stand by it unquestioningly, we would fail to pay attention to concrete history, a failure that is the bogeyman of our essay. If thirty years ago we could hardly contradict Hays's opinion—in 1941 Waldo Frank could write that Spanish-language poets were, "by far the finest company of poets in the world today"[47]—writers such as the Cuban Alejo Carpentier and the Peruvian José María Arguedas, had begun the broadening out of the Latin-American novel[48] that, several decades later would culminate in those "great examples of Latin-American novel writing" that Schnelle and so many others have observed. Of course, it is not just a matter of literary change—a matter on which Alejo Carpentier himself would theorize acutely.[49] Hays conjectured that the "superiority of poetry in Spanish American literature seems to be due in part to the feudal mixture of great masses with the leavening of a small intellectual minority," whereas "in world literature, the full development of the novel seems to coincide with the complex integration of industrial society."[50] Schnelle posing questions about "the period, historically speaking" to which the new Latin-American novel belongs, responds, "to the period of Latin-American national liberation, the revolutionary period, which is also that of bourgeois national revolutions, in a word, the period in which present-day Latin American literary history lives."[51] Dessau, furthermore, takes the view that the "recent surge of the Latin-American novel is conditioned by the way it approaches both the past and the future as problems of individuals and peoples who, through a variety of forms of consciousness, forge their own history."[52] We do not necesssarily have to accept Lucien Goldmann's idea of symmetrical homologies between the so-called *nouveau roman* in France and post–World War II French capitalist society.[53] Only by making manifest the relation between literature and social class in our America—a task still facing us—will we be able to explain thoroughly the singular fact that the Spanish-American novel, which (along with the theater) habitually had been the poor relative of our letters, has so distinguished itself in recent years, years that have witnessed the rise and development of the first socialist revolution in America, the beginning of the weakening of North American imperialism, and the growth of nationalist affirmation in our countries.

A theory of literature cannot fail to consider that literature's theory of history and its theory of criticism as well. As Rita Schober has rightly said when speaking of periodization—a central problem of literary history (to which I shall return later on)—the problem "does not so much concern the limited field of literary history as it does that of literary theory in general."[54] Discussing the link between the two disciplines, history and criticism, Lunacharski, in part 3 of his "Thesis on the tasks of Marxist criticism," explained:

> We often distinguish between the tasks of the critic and those of the literary historian, and when we do, we draw a line between the study of the past and that of the present, as we do likewise between the objective study of a given work, its place in the social fabric, its influence on social life—the literary historian's task—and the critical judgment of a given work from the point of view of its formal and social virtues and defects—the critic's task. For the Marxist critic, such a division is virtually without merit.[55]

I think it is vital to affirm this criterion energetically against para-formalist ahistoricism. Literary history and criticism are two sides of the same coin: a literary history without critical judgment is unrealizable; similarly, a criticism cut off from history is useless or insufficient (just as both are essentially related to literary theory). If each has specific features, those features do not divide or disunite them, because both disciplines feed on one another. This is the view that the Colombian scholar Carlos Rincón, took in "Sobre crítica y historia de la literatura hoy en Hispanoamerica" [On Literary Criticism and Literary History in Spanish America][56] a notable exposition of many of the problems facing both disciplines at present. I will pose here a few questions that Rincón has barely touched on in his essay, most especially the matter of periodization.

Just as when referring to the fundamental genres of our literature, we were concerned not with pursuing *invented* genres, but instead with showing how certain ones *predominated* and how they formed hierarchies and interrelationships in Spanish America, we will best proceed in similar fashion in discussing the periods of our literary history. Although some work has been published on this subject, more often than not it poses metropolitan or "general" problems.[57] For this reason, José Antonio Portuondo's study " 'Períodos' y 'generaciones' en la historiografía literaria hispanoamericana" ['Periods' and 'generations' in Spanish-American literary historiography] is particularly important.[58] In it the author examines the main periodization devices that had been proposed for our literature up to the year of his essay (1947)—strangely, he omits the important one that

Mariátegui proposed in his *Siete ensayos*[59]—and concludes with a new proposal. For Portuondo, Pedro Henríquez Ureña in his *Corrientes literarias en la América hispánica* [Literary Currents in Hispanic America] "accomplished the task of writing the history of Spanish-American letters as a narration of the efforts of generation after generation in search of our own forms of expression," And he adds, "That is surely the best direction, perhaps the only direction, for Spanish-American literary historiography to take,"(90); furthermore, "now it is far easier for us to grasp the autonomy of literature without ignoring its close relationship to all other facets of cultural life." (91). Finally, Portuondo suggests his own schema of periodization (eight periods—from "The Discovery and Conquest [1492–1600]" to "Proletarianism and Purism [1916–19–]"), which he explains thusly:

> In the chronological division that we propose, each period is
> characterized by the predominance of a particular literary attitude or
> tendency, but there is still room for isolated individuals and groups that
> might have no place in the major generational units . . . We have tried
> in every instance to show the simultaneous presence of the historical
> continuity of our letters together with what we have described as the
> dialectical play of populists and formalists in each period. The terms
> used to characterize periods are inherent in their content. In any event,
> our periodological essay aspires mainly to propose a subject of
> discussion for historians of Spanish-American literature and specialists
> in literary theory. [98–99]

In the book published in 1958 in which this study was collected, Portuondo added an "Esquema de las generaciones literarias cubanas" [An Overview of Cuban Literary Generations], the first part of which complemented the earlier piece and commented on Enrique Anderson Imbert's periodization, which in Portuondo's view supersedes "most of our chronological indecisiveness and our 1947 periodization."[60] Anderson Imbert makes use of the generational method, which Portuondo also employed, albeit calling into question its reactionary use.[61] Rincón, on the other hand, is implacable in his judgment of that method and Anderson Imbert's use of it:

> There is, above all, an unquestionable fact that casts doubt on the
> idealist generational criterion as a periodizing principle. A "generational
> consciousness" has proved possible only since the establishment of
> bourgeois society in Europe . . . In other words, under the ancien
> régime—which still existed in most of Latin America until the late
> nineteenth century—no such generational consciousness as a correlative
> of a new literary style could possibly arise . . . Thus, we have no right
> to use the term retroactively. ["CHL," 145 n. 53]

Since Portuondo plainly did not share this view in his 1958 volume, he offered still another provisional periodization that followed a strict generational division, explaining: "The development of the overview, which at present is simply a project, will be the subject of further research that, at present is underway"(100). Unfortunately, Portuondo—one of the few people capable of the undertaking— has not yet done it. Rincón, moreover, does not offer us a working hypothesis and concludes with these words: "[T]he work that remains cannot conceivably be accomplished outside the context of broadly collective work" ("CHL," 147).

For the accomplishment of this necessary task, the material presented in Prague at the 1966 International Colloquium on Problems of Periodization in Literary History is of capital importance. Although nominally on French literature, it went far beyond those bounds and offered ideas that plainly are of use to us. As the Czech professor Jan O. Fischer stated in his opening remarks: "[W]e decided to begin with general methodological problems, go on to the particular concerns of French literary history . . . ,and conclude with problems of comparative and world literature."[62]

Since it is impossible to make a précis of all the papers, we will concentrate on two that we deem particularly important to us, the essays by the Czech professor Oldřich Bělič[63] and the Soviet researcher Zlata Potapova. Bělič's central points are:

1. "The basis of a good method of periodization will . . . necessarily be empirical . . . And the characteristics and symptoms discovered empirically will, by this method, become criteria" (18).
2. "If we succeed in defining the 'methodological' idea or concept of a period, we cannot turn it into an abstract model, a pattern, to be applied mechanically to any and all literature" (19).
3. "I cannot deny the existence and the importance of immanent factors . . . But I am convinced that the leading role belongs to extraliterary motor forces" (19).
4. "We must use exclusively literary criteria to reveal and describe the evolution of literature; to explain it, we necessarily must have recourse to extraliterary factors" (20).
5. On the "names of periods":
   a "The names of periods are nothing but labels."
   b "We must avoid the confusion between periodization and names. What always matters is periodization."
   c "Regarding the practical solution to the problem, I think that we should keep names wherever their use has been agreed upon by custom. And where they do not exist, it would be advantageous to link literature through period names to other activities of the social group in question, especially historical activities" (21).

To these observations, of general validity, we should add those offered by Zlata Potapova in "Algunos principios generales sobre la periodización en la *Historia de la literatura mundial* (sobre todo en los volúmenes consagrados a los siglos XIX y XX)" [Some General Principles of Periodization in the *History of World Literature* (With Particular Reference to the Volumes on the Nineteenth and Twentieth Centuries)], where she discusses the history of world literature that the USSR's Maxim Gorky Institute of World Literature is preparing.[64] In Potapova's view, after "describing the tenencies which determine the literary process in the historical development of national literatures" (68), "the second important feature" of the *History* "is the authors' desire and the duty to show the parallel development of literatures the world over as they free themselves from the principle of Eurocentrism in the analysis of their material." To this end, "it is absolutely indispensable to work out a periodization that would be valid for the West as well as for the East, thus enabling us to grasp the general laws of world literary development on a given historical basis for, let us say, Russia and Latin America" (69). Further on she states, "[H]istorical periodization should be a step toward a general theory of international processes, since the very notion of 'world literature' is linked to them" (69); although she later [*or* soon] qualifies this by acknowledging, "I must confess that we have not yet worked out a unified and perfectly valid concept" (70).

With this kind of work as our starting point, we must return to the periodization of our literary history. Although such periodization must always be faithful to our specific characteristics and therefore will, as Bělič rightly says, "necessarily be empirical," nevertheless it must, in accordance with Potopova's view, take into account our link to the rest of the world. The "periods" of our literary history must unequivocally be ours, but can they be so to such an extent that they will bear no relation to the "periods" of the literary histories of the countries with which we have had close ties or whose social structure is quite similar to our own? Of course not. They will be ours because they will imply a particular kind of link to the rest of the world, because they will be instances of our way of being in the world. Our colonial origins, our subsequent neocolonial process, our complex and difficult configurations through our own history make periodization an arduous task. We cannot simply substitute a fierce, naive tabula rasa for metropolitan categories and periods. We need concrete research and careful delimitation of the problem, and that is the task we have undertaken. While, for example, our "modernismo" has long been the object of heated polemics,[65] in recent times so has our "baroque" and our "romanticism." With respect to the former, as against certain equivocal interpretations, Leonardo Acosta states that the baroque, taken in a precise historical sense, was

> a style imported by the Spanish monarchy as part of a culture closely connected to imperialist ideology. From the very outset, its importation

served the purpose of ideological and cultural domination. This does not imply a negative aesthetic judgment. But we do believe it necessary to be aware both of the true meaning of the baroque, which is a strictly European phenomenon, and of the need to develop our own artistic forms in this stage of Latin America's economic, political and cultural liberation, forms that in many regards will be the contrary of the baroque.[66]

Concerning romanticism, Federico Alvarez, for whom it is a "question . . . closely related to the national consciousness of the bourgeoisie," observes:

[R]efusing to deploy nineteenth-century European literary periodizations in a mechanistic way, I defend the idea that, beginning with the period of Independence, the incipient Spanish-American bourgeoisie expresses itself literarily within the framework of a broad *eclecticism,* from which the higher-reaching, progressive, social *realism* of our greatest nineteenth-century writers soon emerges. What develops simultaneously is a broadly inclusive, chaotic movement of servile imitation of European romantic models, a collection of pastiches . . . and, finally, a full-blooded romanticism, a necessarily late and highly mitigated arrrival (in the last third of the century) [of which, for this observer, *Tabaré (1888)* is a good example].[67]

Mirta Aguirre, for her part, does not doubt "the existence of a Latin American Romanticism—it is plainly visible—although we do not lack for critics who would rather deny it because it is not a perfect reproduction of the European model."[68] Nevertheless, it might be possible to find an area of agreement between the two critics if we observe that when Alvarez speaks of resistence to the "mechanistic deployment of nineteenth-century *European* literary periodizations," he clearly has in mind the Western "Europe" of capitalist development rather than the *other,* peripheral Europe, where, Mirta Aguirre tells us, "in the socially and economically most backward countries—Poland, Hungary . . . — there was a rapprochement of literature and politics in which romanticism was, in fact, fused with the patriotic impulse toward national liberty, in much the same way as in Italy"(26). And further: "[T]here were romantics whose ideas were more or less backward and others who were rather more forward-looking. The latter can be found less often in France than in Italy, in Poland, in Hungary, or in the pre-Decembrist period in Russia, where the surge of romanticism coincided with the struggle against feudalism for national independence"(411). Plainly, that *other* romanticism, that of the European *other,* "the socially and economically most backward countries," that romanticism that was "fused with the patriotic impulse toward national liberty," which "coincided with the struggle against feudalism and for national independence," is the one we can compare with *our* romanticism. Then it will be permissible to accept the term without feeling that we are mechanically "deploy[ing] nineteenth-century European literary periodizations."

Literary Criticism

Martí, ever faithful to etymology, would state repeatedly that "criticism is the employment of criteria." That definition, as modest as it is beyond reproach, leads us to new questions: What criteria? Does value-free criticism make sense? If we are to judge, how shall we arrive at a hierarchy of values? Is it possible— or desirable—to make exclusively aesthetic judgments? Of course, we cannot simply give answers to these questions, but neither can we avoid their polemical thrust.

In the first place, one thing is evident: criticism can be written with whatever set of criteria we choose, but not all criteria are equally admissible. For us there is an immediate dividing line: the criticism of colonialized people, colonialized criticism, is not only incapable of accounting for our letters but rather, in more or less conscious fashion, performs a harmful task in distorting the evaluation of a literature whose chief merit is precisely its contribution to the expression and even the affirmation of our being. In this category must be included the militant, purely colonialized critics—those who scavenge the theoretical leftovers that fall from the West's dinner table and apply them unthinkingly—along with the impure, or more malicious, colonials. We needn't bother with names, which, thanks to some rather predictable publishing strategies, are well known. But even honest people who could never be confused with the former are in partial agreement with them when they call for a "Che Guevara of language." Che's works—his speeches, testimonies, articles, letters, his diary—belong to the main line of Spanish American literature that we already discussed: thus, the Che Guevara of language proper to our America is . . . Che Guevara. That expression, in clearer prose, takes up the colonialized critics' thesis. It amounts to a demand, returning to Szabolsci's words, to blow up the linguistic "outer shell" of our spoken Spanish, just as certain French bourgeois writers have been doing for some time. But what is characteristic, what is exemplary, in Che Guevara is precisely that he does not give in to the colonials' demands either in politics or in writing, and that is what makes him who he is. A "Che Guevara of language" would have the slight disadvantage of bearing no resemblance to Che Guevara or, by extension, to our America. Naturally, we would not propose the meek acceptance of received language, and I am not unaware of the differences among distinct literary genres (testimony, the novel, poetry, for example), but it was not we who introduced that unhappy metaphor. In short, only decolonialzed points of view will allow us to do justice to our letters.

Moreover, a value-free criticism of the kind Jakobson recommends and many critics say they write has, in our view, two defects, one general, the other partic- ular. Although a precise description of a literary work's structures is undoubtedly interesting and useful, the fact that it is done without reference to the work's value means that we are performing a critical task on an object that could as eas- ily merit our admiration as our indifference, or even our censure. In fact, how- ever, that so-called criticism without criteria, that throws judgment out the door, brings it back in through the window. The criterion of judgement operates in the choice of the object of our attention and is implicit in the choice itself; it is to be expected that the "critic" who feels the discussion of that fact beneath him cheerfully intends to impose his decision on us. We may presuppose that the work is good, he seems to be telling us, and the proof, if any is needed, is that he is working on it.

Nonetheless, does not this kind of criticism, so thoroughly determined to all appearances by linguistics (actually colonized by it), possess the irrefutable rigor of science? Have we not at last reached the point of strictly scientific study of the literary work? This is not the first time that one discipline, having been colonized by another one, has suffered such ravages. For example, the mechanical extrap- olation to human history of Darwin's discoveries in natural science lamentably allowed racists to marshall ostemsibly scientific "facts" in support of their ideas. When Sarmiento, or some of the leading lights of Mexican positivism, or Ingenieros defended their rampant racism, they believed that they were operating on a solid scientific foundation.[69] They were unaware that "races" are basically a historical phenomenon, not a biological one and that, consequently, history cannot be understood with the imported assistance of a *different* science while its own concrete, specific problem is ignored. When in our own day literary scholars colonized by linguistics proudly proclaim the scientific nature of their undertak- ing, they merely flourish pseudoscientific arguments for their neo-rhetorical labors — useful, no doubt, though modest and of course acritical or at very best precritical.

Linguistics, the *purpose* of which is the study of language, is for that very reason anaxological; literary criticism, on the other hand, works with literary works, whose *medium* is language, and to declare it anaxological is to deprive it of ultimate meaning. Naturally, we can do a *linguistic* study of a literary text to very good effect, and we can do likewise with a juridical or historical text: but if the first study is *already* literary criticism, then the second belongs to jurispru- dence, and the third to historiography, which, frankly, does not strike us as very defensible. The truth is that literary criticism *colonized* by linguistics (which should not be confused with criticism *enriched* by it) is no more scientific than the racism supported by the crude colonization of history by natural science. In each case we are in the presence of pseudoscientific, characteristically ideologi- cal realities, taking ideology in the Marxist sense of false consciousness. Of course, this reductio ad absurdum should not blind us to the essential difference between those two ideological forms, a difference based on the fact that racism is anti-scientific in its entirety, whereas in the case of criticism invaded by linguistics, the antiscientific aspect (as I shall have occasion to reiterate) is in linguistics' attempt to exceed the function it can and should perform as an auxiliary method of criticism, rather than as a substitute for it.

But if this seems to us to be the defect of a science attempting to transgress its own bounds no matter what the cost, doing so with a literature like ours makes things even worse. Metropolitan literatures are refined by a lengthy process of distillation that, although it does not exclude the need for rethinking,[70] allows for an ease, a confidence, that we rarely possess. The encounter, not of the proverbial umbrella with the proverbial sewing machine but rather with a harsh, indeterminate reality such as ours, with conceptual tools that often are inadequate, surely has not made a coherent understanding (or even a mere appreciation) of our letters any easier. The way out of this tangle certainly cannot be to suspend our minds (which, in our case, would be tantamount to losing them), but rather to use them rigorously and without either self-satisfaction or submissiveness. And certainly we must have recourse to our own set of values born of the grasp of our literature's specificities—not necessarily of what separates it from other literatures, surely not of what within it that is dead weight, pastiche, the mimetic echo of metropolitan achievements, but rather—as Mariátegui had demanded of our political life—its "heroic creation," our true contribution to the attainments of humankind.

Pedro Henríquez Ureña long ago pointed out how necessary it is for us to "put sets of values into circulation: centrally important names and indispensable books"[71] Those values can only be a broad, general view of what is most authentic in our literature, encarnate in its works, and the best demonstration of that generalization are the works themselves, which Henríquez Ureña urged be "put . . . into circulation." The situation was far more serious in 1925, when those words were written, than in our own time. Back then, Henríquez Ureña could mention only two "attempts to constitute a library of Spanish-American classics"—one by Rufino Blanco Fombona and Ventura Garca Calderón. In recent years, there has been considerable growth in the circulation of high quality texts of Spanish-American literature. With regard to the classics, we need only mention the *Biblioteca Americana* [The (Latin) American Library] published in Mexico by Fondo de Cultura Económica, exemplary in the rigorousness of its selections and editions, which originally was Pedro Henríquez Ureña's project and was published in his memory, and, with the inclusion of more recent texts, Casa de las Américas's *Colección Literatura Latinoamericana* [The Latin-American Literature Collection].[72] Furthermore, it is significant that whereas in the nineteenth century, and even when Pedro Henríquez Ureña brought out his *Seis ensayos en busca de nuestra expresión* [Six Essays in Search of Our Own Forms of Expression] (1928), a book of capital importance, it was common for our writers to have to publish in a metropolitan country (as it still is for writers from the non-Spanish-speaking Antilles), most Ibero-American countries now publish the great majority of their own works and have done so for some time.

However, if "showing off" literary works is essential, let us not forget that it is no substitute for critical and theoretical discussion, because only such discussion can lead to the selection and hierarchization of those works. It is true that values are incarnate in works, and an axiological approach simply makes them manifest. But such an approach is essential, because if it is indeed able to reveal actual values, it makes it possible for us to picture an authentic and coherent literary world, bringing certain works into proximity with one another and separating them from others, highlighting certain of the formers' essential characteristics and distinguishing the works which merit the broad circulation Henríquez Ureña demanded. This is a complex operation or, more precisely, several operations, and if some of them are, by their very nature, theoretical and critical, the task of "put[ting] . . . into circulation . . . centrally important names and indispensable books" is, in essence, neither: it is (we cannot shun the term) a *political* task proper to cultural politics, which necessarily looks to the other politics (in the broadest sense) within which it has specific functions. Those collections of major works of Spanish-American literature fully exemplify this fact. Unfortunately, no less an exemplification is the tendentious utilization of a trend in recent Spanish-American narrative, that came to be called by the disagreeable name of "the boom," promoted for political and business reasons.[73] The connections between a certain ahistoricizing criticism and that promotional effort are obvious, and so it is absurd to look at both of them through exclusively, technically "literary" glasses. The argument over them must also—and, at times, especially— take other motives into account.

Assuming that literary judgment is indispensable and taking facts like those just pointed out into consideration, it seems to me that on the matter of the criteria that our criticism requires—and, if you like, the urgency of the critical undertaking—Reyes remarks are still valid:

> So-called pure—aesthetic and stylistic [today we would say
> para-formalist or structuralist]—criticism takes nothing other than the
> specifically literary value of a work's form and content into
> consideration. But it could not lead to a fully rounded judgment or
> understanding. If we do not take social, historical, biographical or
> psychological factors into account, we will not arrive at a just
> evaluation.[74]

The demand for what Reyes elsewhere called "methodological integration" and what today might better be termed "interdisciplinary collaboration"—which should never be confused with brainless eclecticism—has been expounded in our time by the Mexican critic Jaime Labastida:

> We must avoid . . . two false paths toward the solution of the artistic
> question: one would be the reduction of the work to its (economic,
> political, social) signifieds, with which we would succumb to the vice
> of vulgar sociologism or economism; the other path would be
> represented by the formalist claim to find nothing in the work beyond a
> purely formal order (signifiers), more recently, the reproduction of
> linguistic models, the *parole* of the novelists' *écriture*. The correct
> method would seem, on the contrary, to be the noneclectic union of the
> best of both tendencies or attempted solutions.[75]

No doubt we will get the criticism we need by integrating the best of each
method and avoiding the pitfalls of both We are already well acquainted with one
of the pitfalls and today on every side critics rival each other in denigrating it
(significantly, among those who do so most enthusiastically are yesterday's most
intransigent practitioners): it is *vulgar sociologism*. But we should reject the
other pitfall no less energetically, and we can easily suggest a symmetrical label
for it: *vulgar structuralism*. This second pitfall, moreover, is at present the
greater menace, because bourgeois scholarship endeavors to tar every historical
approach with the brush of vulgar sociologism the better to impose its own
ahistoricism.

The rejection of pitfalls, however, cannot at all mean the rejection of the *methods* of which the pitfalls are an exaggerated extrapolation or absolutization.
Without the best of those methods criticism is simply infeasable: for one thing,
they will enable us to forge the links between our works of literature and the real
history of our countries, thus making them fully comprehensible, (even though
that history has still to be written in accord with scientific criteria, a fact that
makes our task considerably more difficult); for another, it will give us a grasp of
the real formal characteristics of our works as well as their conceptual function,
an area where Della Volpe is most helpful.[76] Both, coherently integrated, will
produce the criticism we need to approach our literature in a mature way, for our
literature is itself more mature than its theory and criticism. This however, when
all is said and done, is less alarming than would be the opposite—the predominance of criticism and theory, especially of a *certain kind* of criticism and theory,
over literature itself. We have seen numerous examples of this theory overload in
more than one capitalist country, and it is another instance, although we find the
word quite disagreeable, of decadence. Absent is the soaring critique that heralds
intellectual vigor; instead we find, in Antonio Machado's words, ''the misbegot-
ten bustard's flight'' of Alexandrianism, of Byzantinism, of scholastic ergoti-
zers, of newly (and not so newly) coined rhetoric, in sum, of vulgar structuralism. But if it is always better for literature to scale heights that criticism has not
yet reached, the true sign of health is the illumination of literary praxis, like all
praxis, by its theoretical counterpart, permitting us to make judgments that are on

the same level as their object and to place that object organically and properly within a vaster historical universe.[77]

A Provisional Ending

Throughout the travails of our history there has been no lack of worthy, indeed very worthy, contributions to the collective task of coming to grips with the theoretical facets of our literature. The preceeding pages are a modest addition to that undertaking. From the Bello-Sarmiento polemic to the founding work of José Martí; from the indispensable studies of Henríquez Ureña and Alfonso Reyes to the present day, these contributions are a corpus that, to a considerable extent, still awaits a proper evaluation, articulation, and utilization. José Carlos Mariátegui opened a decisive chapter in the history of those ideas with the introduction of Marxism-Leninism into our literary studies. His work has been continued by critics like José Antonio Portuondo and a fine group of young scholars from every area of our continent, along with non-Latin-American Marxist scholars (particularly those from the socialist countries), they all, especially in recent years (beginning with the victory of the Cuban Revolution and the attention it attracted toward our America) have made important contributions. Together with those who will follow them, they are clearing the terrain so that eventually we can work out a theory that is adequate to our letters. That we have a long way to go should not cause us to lose heart. Jean Pérus considers literary theory in general "an emerging science," and he speaks of its "uncertain status";[78] and in its presentation of the essay "Une science du littéraire: Est-elle possible?" [Is a Literary Science Possible?], the French Communist journal *La nouvelle critique,* states that "we have not yet done the work that will form the basis of a Marxist theory of the phenomenon of literature."[79] Perhaps this is a bit exaggerated,[80] but as nearly as we can tell, and despite the tangle of our history, *in a certain sense* we are in circumstances similar to everyone elses', with all due consideration to each particular case. Accordingly, our insistence in rejecting the indiscriminate imposition of criteria born of other literatures cannot in any way be construed as isolationism: the truth is the exact opposite. We need to think out our concrete reality and point out its specific features, because this is the only way we will discover what we have in common with every other area of the globe, detect the real links, and arrive at what, someday, truly will be a general theory of world literature.

Prologue to Ernesto Cardenal

In 1949 an event of great importance to Spanish poetry took place: in that year the anthology *New Nicaraguan Poetry* was published in Madrid.[1] Nevertheless, it is interesting that the event, like so many similar ones, was noteworthy only in that hardly anyone took note of it. Nowadays—a nowadays that encompasses many years—things are very different. It has been well known for some time that the poetry written in Nicaragua—a small country with fewer inhabitants than the average city in either Latin America itself or worldwide—is some of the best being written not only in Latin America but perhaps worldwide. Add to this another remarkable fact—if on the eve of the First World War, a person knowledgeable about Spanish poetry had been asked to name the most influential living poet writing in Spanish, the answer without a doubt would have been: the Nicaraguan Rubén Darío. Today, we trust, *not* on the eve of the Third (and last) World War, and taking for granted that men such as Vicente Aleixandre, Rafael Alberti, and Nicolás Guillen are already considered to be living classics, I think that a similar question would be answered: the Nicaraguan Ernesto Cardenal. That is to say, in the twentieth century (even though there are still a few years left to ratify or rectify this statement) poetry written in the Spanish language began and ended—in

---

I wrote this text in 1981, at the request of Angel Rama, as a prologue to an anthology of Ernesto Cardenal's poetry that was to have been published by Stockholm's Forlaget Norden. I do not know what became of that book after Rama's tragic death. Moreover, Cardenal has subsequently published other books, on which, for obvious chronological reasons, I have nothing to say in this essay.—Author's note, 1985.

short, was led—by two Nicaraguan poets, on the one end, Rubén Darío and, on the other, Ernesto Cardenal.

In 1957 I still had not perceived this. In that year, when I gave a lecture at Columbia University in New York on "The Present State of Spanish-American Poetry," I was already aware of how important the new poetry being written in Nicaragua was.[2] But when I went to choose a representative name from the then-younger generation of that country's poets, I chose Ernesto Mejía Sánchez. I have no regrets, for he is an excellent poet; Cardenal, on the other hand, was still untried and had not yet published his first book. The 1949 anthology included three of his poems, well-written ones, but ones that he himself would leave out of later collections.[3] He also was the author of the anthology's long prologue, in which he declared: "We cannot explain [Rubén] Darío, but we can state that if Nicaragua ever gives another writer to world literature and it is not [José] Coronel Urtecho, it will be due to him."[4] It has indeed turned out that way. Coronel Urtecho's reputation is based on his special role as a poet-docent. He is a man who has produced not books of poetry—at age seventy-five he has had only one book published—but poets. The most famous of all, the other Nicaraguan name to take its place in world literature, is Ernesto Cardenal.

In 1960 I received a copy personally sent by him (as I would of his later publications) of a work that moved me greatly. It was *Hora O* [Zero Hour], a collection of four poems centered around the theme of the struggle for national liberation in Central America, especially Nicaragua's struggle. It included an unforgettable evocation of Sandino, the great Nicaraguan hero of the anti-Yankee resistance who was assassinated by the first Somoza in 1934. The colophon, almost certainly written by Mejía Sánchez explained:

> These poems by Ernesto Cardenal, *Hora O,* were written in Nicaragua between the time of the April 1954 rebellion, in which the author took part, and the political execution of the dictator Anastasio Somoza on 21 September 1956. Later on, Ernesto Cardenal turned to religion, entering the Trappist monastery of Our Lady of Gethsemane in Kentucky. From there he authorized the publication of *Hora O* in the *Revista Mexicana de Literatura* [Mexican Review of Literature], nos. 9 and 10 (January–April 1957) and no. 2 (April–June 1959). After being transferred to the Benedictine monastery of Saint Mary of the Resurrection in Cuernavaca, Morelos, for reasons of health, Cardenal authorized this complete edition as an homage to the hero Augusto César Sandino, on the twenty-sixth anniversary of his death, 21 February 1960.[5]

This colophon, virtually an essay, tells us a good many things and makes reference to other important information. To begin with, it becomes clear that this poet, born in 1925 in Granada into a wealthy family and brought up in León,

Nicaragua—the city of Rubén Darío's childhood—had already lived an unusual life. Along with receiving an education befitting a young man of the Central American upper bourgeoisie (not only the schooling he received in his own country but also the training in the humanities that he received in Mexico, the United States, and Spain) and writing numerous poems from childhood on (which he did not bother to gather into a book)—up to this point, nothing out of the ordinary— it must be added that in 1954 he participated in a conspiracy to execute the aged tyrant Somoza. This laudable project failed at the last minute; the conspirators were viciously hunted down, and most of them were annihilated. Cardenal managed to save his life by going into hiding. In 1956 another poet, Rigoberto López Pérez, would put Somoza I to death and pay for the deed with his own instant assassination. Shortly thereafter, Cardenal, who almost simultaneously had been writing lyric and political epigrams, translating Catullus and Martial, and working on *Hora O*, underwent an intense religious crisis and decided to become a priest. The great poet and Trappist monk Thomas Merton granted him admission to the monastery of Our Lady of Gethsemane, Kentucky. In 1957 Cardenal entered the novitiate under the name of M. Lawrence. In the monastery he was prohibited from writing poetry, but he took notes that later he would turn into poems.

The austerity of the Trappists' life is well known. What is not so well known is that Merton urged them to pray for the safety of Fidel Castro and the rebels in the Sierra Maestra in Cuba (a country he knew well and to which he devoted many beautiful pages in his books *The Seven Storey Mountain* and *The Secular Journey*) when he got word of the revolution's victory in 1959. In the same year, having moved to the monastery at Cuernavaca for reasons of health, as Mejía Sánchez mentions, Cardenal put the finishing touches on the poems in his notebook entitled *Gethsemane, Kentucky* (published in Mexico with a prologue by Merton in 1960).[6] And he authorized the publication of two collections of earlier poems, the aforementioned *Hora O* (1960) and the *Epigramas* [Epigrams] (1961). The unsigned introduction to the latter volume was also written by [Ernesto] Mejía Sánchez, who has turned out to be one of most acute (anonymous) heralds of his namesake and "inevitable fellow countryman."[7] The author of the introduction describes Cardenal's poetic evolution in this way:

> He began by writing youthful love poems, and there was even a title advertised as forthcoming, *Carmen y otros poemas* ["Carmen" and Other Poems]. He continued to write and, without leaving aside the theme of love, began to develop historical subjects in such poems as "Raleigh" and "Walker." He eventually arrived at the brevity of the epigram, social and political poetry and once again, Christian love, religious love. Many stages in twenty years, many dispersed poems, and only two published notebooks: *Hora O* and *Gethsemane, Kentucky*. The first is political poetry, passionate, virile, against his country's

injustices. The latter is based on his religious experience in the Trappist monastery. . . . [Cardenal] thoroughly devoted himself to a religious and intellectual life. He worked tirelessly on long historical poems, reworking pre-Hispanic literary sources, the chronicles of the conquest, documents from the colonial period.[8]

In the same year he published the *Epigrams,* 1961, Cardenal moved to Christ the Priest Seminary in La Ceja, Antioquia, Colombia (home of the famous priest and guerrilla fighter Camilo Torres) where he studied theology. In Colombia he published two new books: *Salmos* [Psalms] (1964) and *"Oración por Marilyn Monroe" y otros poemas* ["Prayer for Marilyn Monroe" and Other Poems] (1965). Even then, despite the brevity of his published work, he was undoubtedly one of the most important Spanish-American poets of the day.

On his return to Nicaragua he became a priest, receiving the sacrament of holy orders in Managua on 15 August 1964. A few months later, he announced to his friends in his "Letter from Solentiname," which I received in mimeograph, that on Sunday, 13 February 1966 (two days before the death of Father Camilo Torres in the guerrilla struggle in Colombia) he had arrived at "the islands of Solintiname," the tiny archipelago on the great Lake Nicaragua, almost entirely cut off from the outside world. On one of these islands, Mancarrón, he founded a contemplative community, "in order to commune with the author of these creatures and of Life, which Saint John tells us, is none other than Love itself." Making a clearing in the thick undergrowth with the help of two Colombian co-workers, he and they built a handful of modest shelters encircling a small church. The few inhabitants of the region, "have come joyfully in their canoes from all the islands to hear mass." But since most of them did not know how to read, the first step of the liturgical movement would be to teach basic literacy to the people of the Archipelago of Solentiname, just as, of necessity, Ash Wednesday sermon was to be on the subject of latrines. "The truth," Cardenal goes on, "is that in order to teach the children the catechism, we must begin by making certain that the children don't die." And elsewhere he says, "Our starting point must be the base." One of the most meaningful spiritual experiences of our time had begun, one that would last twelve years and that from its inception would have unforeseen consequences.

In that year of 1966, Cardenal's book *El estrecho dudoso* [The Uncertain Strait] was published in Madrid with a long, handwritten, utterly immense prologue by Coronel Urtecho. The subject matter was, in the words of the introduction to the *Epigrams,* "those great historical poems" which Cardenal had reworked in Mexico from an acid modernizing viewpoint, "the chronicles of the conquest, the colonial document." Three years later, in 1969, in León, Nicaragua, Cardenal pubished the poetic cycle *Homenaje a los indios americanos* [Homage to the American Indians], which is closely linked to his previous book.

In *El estrecho dudoso* Cardenal makes use of the conquistadors' own texts, taking them apart and reconstructing them (as Archibald MacLeish had done in 1932 in his great poem *Conquistador,* a poem that profoundly influenced Cardenal), and depicting in all its horror the effect of that army with its "white man's burden" upon our lands (and especially upon the "uncertain strait" itself, the passage between the two oceans that was sought in what today is Nicaragua). In *Homage* Cardenal takes the "point of view of the conquered," following the title of the Mexican classic by Miguel León Portilla. He evokes the harmonious world of the true *discoverers* of our continent, the inappropriately named "American Indian," and he shows their destruction, which continue today, by their Western predators, although he does not avoid pointing out in either book the men or circumstances of a different stripe, such as Las Casas or Mayapán. Later, Cardenal wrote many more poems, and at least two—*Canto nacional* [Nicaraguan Canto] and *Oráculo sobre Managua* [Managua Oracle]—would come out as chapbooks, but *Homage to the American Indians* is the last real *book* of poetry he had published up to this point. In 1970 he published in Buenos Aires his first book of prose, *Vida en el amor* [Life in Love], however, a mystical meditation written in the monastery in Cuernavaca, also with a prologue by Merton.

The year 1970 was enormously important in Cardenal's life. Invited by the Casa de las Américas to serve on the jury of its annual literature prize, Cardenal visited revolutionary Cuba for the first time. Thus we were able to meet at last after years of correspondence. For a number of reasons Cardenal found himself in a good position to understand the Cuban Revolution, even though ostensibly the revolution would have more to say to a Marxist-Leninist than to a Christian. It is true, though, that when certain reactionary sectors of the Cuban Catholic church had tried to turn the faithful against the revolution in 1959, Fidel had said that whoever was against the poor was against Christ. Thus began the process of rapprochement that gradually fused Christian revolutionaries and revolutionary socialists, an ongoing process that would be expressed in the ideas brought together under the rubric of "liberation theology," an area in which Cardenal would play a very important role.

> My experience in Cuba [he would state in an interview in 1971 and reiterate later on] created a fundamental change in me. It became the most important experience of my life after my religious conversion. . . . In truth, it was a conversion to the revolution. Before, I thought we should look for a third road in Latin America, but in Cuba I discovered that their road was mine and that their revolution was a very good one and that it must be supported.[9]

From that visit, and from another one he would make the following year, "a much shorter one, for the purpose of talking to Fidel," would come one of the most convincing books of testimonials written on the Cuban Revolution: *En*

Cuba [In Cuba] (1972). Besides a collage of diverse texts, Cardenal brought together everything he saw and everything he was told, including adverse comments. He personally tested out the veracity of each of these criticisms. In 1970 he arrived at my house one night before the time set for our meeting. We had no choice but to share our supper with him. Afterward, reading his book, I found out in the chapter "Supper at Retamar's" that he had been told I had certain privileges. He found out for himself that I had been living in the same modest house since long before the victory of the revolution and that I ate what everyone else did. This small personal detail is one example of the simple and effective method he used in writing the book. Sniffing around in everything, like a kind of Father Brown as straightforward and sharp as Chesterton's character (but without priestly garb: just a *contona*—the Nicaraguan peasants' cotton blouse—jeans, sandals, and a black beret covering his flowing white hair), Cardenal took the country's pulse. He didn't like everything, of course; neither do we. He saw not-very-Christian men of the cloth; he saw dogmatic revolutionaries; but he didn't see beggars, or illiteracy, or discrimination, or prostitution, or luxury, or misery, or injustices ignored, because we have none of these things. Wandering around Havana, he remarked to the Uruguayan writer Mario Benedetti: "I have withdrawn from the world to live on an island, because I loathe cities. But this is my city. I now see that I had not withdrawn from the world, only the capitalist world."[10]

Also published in 1972, a long poem revealed Ernesto's transformation: in *Canto nacional* [Nicaraguan Canto], bravely dedicated to the FSLN (Frente Sandinista de Liberación Nacional [Sandinista National Liberation Front]), he returned to the poetic world of *Zero Hour*. He had never left it entirely, but now it was more complex and more incisively class-conscious. He feels himself—he knows himself to be—the voice of his people and traces the rapacious history of the new Yankee conquistadors, invoking the revolutionary process that "comes from the stars" and "what's even more: / a dead Che smiled as though he had just left Hades." With voracious tenderness he names the fauna, the flora, the landscape, and evokes Sandino once more, affirming his faith in struggle, in what surely will be the victorious revolution, and in the fusion of his two beliefs: "Communism or God's kingdom on earth, which amounts to the same thing."

An earthquake that destroyed the center of Managua spurred Cardenal to write another long, intense poem, *Oráculo sobre Managua* [Managua Oracle] (1973). The poet compares the city's center with an extremely poor outlying barrio, Acahualinca ("victims of a permanent seismic shock, there will be no airplanes / bringing canned food to these people, / no medicines, portable shelters, drinking water"); his poem is traversed by young heroes whose "epic is a newspaper that is gone with the wind"; he exhorts, "let the bishops tell the people, these are your oppressors" (just as Monsignor Romero did, paying with his life and becoming a martyr of the Salvadoran Revolution). Once more he becomes the author of *Life in Love,* the man who has read and cited Teilhard de Chardin and exclaims in pages of impassioned love for humankind as it lives on our fragile planet: "And Yahweh said: I am not, I will be. I am who I will be, he said / I am Yahweh, a God who awaits the future / . . . We will know God when there are no Acahualincas." Unexpectedly, the poet, so reluctant to speak of himself, appears: "The hand that penned epigrams of love handled a Madzen."

How could the poet who had forged this powerful admonitory and prophetic voice continue to live apart from the world in his community of Solintiname? The answer is in Cardenal's third book in prose, although, strictly speaking, the work is not entirely his, as he makes plain in the dedication of the copy he sent me: "This book of mine and of the peasants of Solintiname. Homeland or Death. We shall win." I refer to *El evangelio en Solintiname* [The Gospel in Solintiname] (1975). Ernesto explains in the introduction to the book that in his community "on Sunday, instead of a sermon on the gospel, we have a dialogue." And he adds, "The peasants' commentaries are often more profound than many theologians', but they share the gospel's simplicity. There is nothing strange in this: the *evangelium* or 'good tiding' (the good news for the wretched), was written for them by people like them."[11] Indeed, in this astonishing book, which explains clearly why modern slave societies forbid the slaves to know the gospel, we sense that "the history of early Christianity" is alive, for, according to Engels's classical comparison, it has "notable points of resemblance with the modern working-class movement."[12] A reading of this volume leaves rather little room for doubt about the immediate destiny of its pure, fervid commentators. In 1976 Ernesto went before the Second Russell Tribunal to expound before the whole world the horror of the younger Somoza's tyranny, a tyranny that, like the elder Somoza's, had the full backing of the U.S. government. The following year, 1977, several members of the Solintiname community, imbued with its teachings, attacked the military outpost at San Carlos, the nearest town on the archipelago. The survivors of the assault took to the hills and continued the struggle. Somoza's bloody National Guard destroyed Solintiname. Cardenal, tried and convicted in absentia, took refuge in Costa Rica, where he made known his membership in the FSLN. He traveled abroad as an envoy of the FSLN to denounce the Somoza tyranny. In 1978 he returned to Cuba to serve again on the fury of the Casa de las Américas literary prize. It was then that he allowed us to publish "Lo que fue Solintiname (Carta al pueblo de Nicaragua)" [The Meaning of Solintiname (A Letter to the People of Nicaragua)]. This wrenching document, the reverse of the "Letter from Solintiname" written twelve years earlier, concludes: "I have given no thought to the reconstruction of our little community of Solintiname. I think of the far more important task, the task for us all: the reconstruction of the whole country."[13]

The rest is well known: crowning a heroic struggle of several decades, the Nicaraguan people led by the FSLN, overthrew the vile Somoza regime and won total victory on 19 July 1979. Cardenal, who had entered Nicaragua clandestinely on a night flight the previous day—as he would recount in his poem "Luces" [Lights][14] was appointed minister of culture of the government of national reconstruction.

* * *

I suppose I should say something of Cardenal's "poetics," or at least of the provenance and certain characteristics of his poetry. Cardenal himself has been most explicit on this matter. The most visible source of his poetry—which, in another article, I called "conversational"—is the best of modern North American poetry.[15] Some people have expressed their astonishment at the fact that so anti-imperialist a man as Cardenal could acknowledge his debt to that poetry again and again, as though it were possible to identify the "New Poetry" with the rapacious politics of the empire. Surely they must be unaware that, as Juan Ramón Jiménez stated, "Spain and Spanish Amercia owe, in large part, our poetic access to the United States" to José Martí, the first great poet, who was the first consummate anti-imperialist of our America.[16] Nonetheless, Cardenal's point of reference in this matter is neither Martí nor even the attempt in Mexico shortly after 1920 to make a place for North American poetry in Spanish America—an attempt that the acute Mexican poet-critic José Emilio Pacheco called "the other avant-garde,"[17] among the leaders of which was Salomón de la Selva, the bilingual Nicaraguan who was an accomplished poet in English before he was in Spanish. Rather, Cardenal's touchstone is the magisterial figure of the aforementioned José Coronel Urtecho, who, after his return in 1927 from the United States and the foundation of the Avant-Garde Group, became the prime disseminator of North American poets in our countries. After Cardenal himself learned English in the United States, he worked with Coronel Urtecho in 1963 in developing a great anthology of North American poetry translated into Spanish. According to Ernesto, his principal poetic influence has been Ezra Pound. When Benedetti questioned him about the basis of that influence, Cardenal explained:

> Chiefly, it is in making us see that everything can go into poetry; that there are not some subjects or elements that properly belong in prose and others that belong in poetry. Everything that can be said in a short story, or in an essay, or a novel can be said in poetry as well. . . .
> Another of Pound's teachings has been the *ideogram,* the discovery that poetry is written in exactly the same way as the Chinese ideogram, by superimposing images. . . . Pound's is a direct poetry; he counterposes images, two contrary things or two similar things that, when juxtaposed, create a third image. . . . It is also what film does with montage.[18]

Pound's political leanings are well known. They placed him at the polar opposite of what Cardenal's political position eventually would become. But Cardenal uses montage for his own ends. This, of course, is nothing new. For example, from Shklovsky's *ostranenie*, or defamiliarization, which he considered an artistic "technique," Brecht (who, thanks to Sergei Tretyakov, was apprised of Shklovsky's critical contribution) derived his theory of "distantiation," or "alienation," not merely as a technique but as a weapon in the class struggle.[19] Cardenal has done likewise. Superimposing images in the manner of Chinese ideograms or film montage has not been a mere technique for him (Cardenal, like Brecht, while never disregarding its indispensable *quality*, has always had a utilitarian, practical view of literature)[20] but rather a way to make certain facts manifest the better, eventually to contest them, taking as his starting point materials with which his reader is almost surely familiar, at least in part, so that the reader can then fully decode the message. This is why the clarity of Cardenal's poetry is only relative—although he never reaches the degree of difficulty of Pound's poetry. Cardenal calls his poetry and the kind he prefers, whether Nicaraguan or foreign, "exteriorist" poetry, a term that, according to him, was coined by Coronel Urtecho and that Ernesto defines as

> poetry created with images from the outer world, the world we see and touch, the one that, in general, is the specific world of poetry.
> Exteriorism is objective poetry: narrative and anecdotal, made with real life elements and concrete things, with proper nouns, and exact details, and precise data, and fact and figures, and quotes. In a word, it is *impure* poetry.[21]

But "exteriorism," as clearly can be seen in the montage of film images,[22] does not simply offer itself up to us, for it implies the juxtaposition of two images (one of which, in poetry, need not be explicit but must be known in some fashion to the reader) so that a third element can arise *from within the reader*, who thus is required to abandon his passivity when faced with a genuinely *open work*. For example the first edition of Cardenal's *Epigrams*, (1961) includes, in additon to forty-nine original poems, Ernesto's free translations of thirty-four poems by Catullus and thirty-nine by Martial. Although subsequent editions of his collected poetry usually have bypassed this work, it did help to produce better readers of Cardenal's own epigrams. If, on the one hand, Pound interested him in the Latin epigrammatic poets, on the other, what is made manifest in counterpoint to them (as well as to Pound's versions of them) is the Central American poet's different outlook, his "Third World perspective," the way "he looks at things from [a Latin] American shore . . . , sending us back through the servants' entrance to the world of political struggle, to anti-Somozism, that is, antiwealth, antimetropolitanism, anti-imperialism, which is the victory of pro-love and pro-poetry," as Ariel Dorfman has rightly pointed out.[23] In the *Salmos* [Psalms] (1964), updated translations of twenty-five of the 150 psalms of the Book of Psalms come raining down upon the energetically rejected world of modern capitalism and its wars, gangsters, politicos, and petty tyrants like Somoza.[24]

It is not necessary and would almost be offensive to take readers by the hand and guide them through all the examples of Cardenal's poetry: the result of the montage of images, what stamps his texts with the imprint of dramatic gravity, of tense immediacy, is that he makes us live the creation of the cosmos and the apocalypse, the Spanish conquest, the destruction of native cultures, the expansion of Yankee imperialism into our countries, the deceit and cruelty of capitalist society *here and now;* we see rising before our eyes a God who will be and a revolution that comes all the way from the atoms of hydrogen in intergalactic space and is carried forward by Sandino's struggle, by Che, by "the wretched of the earth." In the active reading his poetry demands—and here we can see the author's clear ideological evolution—the universe is real and is now and is beautiful and is love and is struggle.

* * *

A few days after the victory of the Nicaraguan Revolution (and, of course, by virtue of it) I went at last to Nicaragua. Along with Ernesto and a few members of what had been his community (or, as he would call it later on, his commune) at Solintiname—youngsters in soldiers' garb, armed, happy as kids on their outing—I visited what remained of it. In a single-engine plane buffeted by the wind we reached San Carlos. Traces of the 1977 attack were still in evidence on the darkened walls of the National Guard outpost. Later that day we crossed the astonishingly beautiful lake in an old barge and went to the archipelago, to Mancarrón. It was the first time that together—Ernesto, Olivia, Bosco, Alejandro, Nubia, Iván, others; with the memory of Felipe, Elvis, and Donald, fallen in combat or murdered—they had visited the place since they had fled it—some to fight, others into exile—since Somoza's guard had razed it. Tropical undergrowth was reclaiming its land, but the ruins that could be rebuilt remained. Here and there you would find a scorched magazine, a book, a stick of furniture. I looked not so much at the things as at Ernesto's and the others' faces. Twelve years of their lives had been lived in this outback, in contemplation at first, growing toward action born of love and sacrifice later on. So many realities that would turn the world around had been born there: poems, paintings, handicrafts, loves, dreams, the revolution. They have not disappeared. These people know they're alive. Today, Nicaragua is a great Solintiname.

I would like to finish here, with a sort of happy ending. But can I really? As I write these pages, the news is worrisome. The little Solintiname was demolished by Somoza's barbarians. What does it mean to say that Nicaragua today is Solintiname writ large? Will this lovely, impoverished, combative country be able to carry on its projects of putting an end to misery and oppression (it already has put an end to illiteracy) in peace, to build a world of love and justice of which the immense prophetic voice of Ernesto Cardenal cries out? And will we, on the rest of the planet, remain indifferent if Solintiname is once again the victim of aggression? Does anyone have the right to praise the words of the best of men like Cardenal and not keep faith with what those words say? Truly to admire this extraordinary poet requires the defense of his ideals, his people, his poetry, his truth, so that our lives, so that life itself may be meaningful, from the distant stars to the delicate earth-colored girls and boys who today are Ernesto Cardenal's finest poems.

—Havana, 3 December 1981

Notes

Notes

Preface

1. Louis Althusser and Etienne Balibar, *Reading Capital*, trans. Ben Brewster (London, 1970), 14.

Caliban

1. See Yves Lacoste, *Les pays sous-développés* [The Underdeveloped Countries] (Paris, 1959), 82–84.

2. José Vasconcelos, *La raza cósmica* [The Cosmic Race] (1925). A Swedish summary of what is known on this subject can be found in Magnus Mörner's study, *La mezcla de razas en la historia de América Latina*, [The Mixture of Races in the History of Latin America], Jorge Piatigorsky (Buenos Aires, 1969). Here it is recognized that "no part of the world has witnessed such a gigantic mixing of races as the one that has been taking place in Latin America and the Caribbean [Why this division?] since 1492" (15). Of course, what interests me in these notes is not the irrelevant biological fact of the "races" but the historical fact of the "cultures"; see Claude Lévi-Strauss, *Race et histoire* [Race and History] [1952] (Paris, 1968).

3. Cited along with subsequent references to the *Diario* [Logbook], by Julio C. Salas, in *Etnografía americana: Los indios caribes — Estudio sobre el origen del mito de la antropofagia* [Latin-American Ethnography: The Carib Indians — A Study of the Origin of the Myth of Anthropophagy] (Madrid, 1920). The book exposes "the irrationality of [the] charge that some American tribes devoured human flesh, maintained in the past by those interested in enslaving [the] Indians and repeated by the chroniclers and historians, many of whom were supporters of slavery" (211).

4. *La carta de Colón anunciando el descubrimiento del nuevo mundo, 15 de febrero — 14 de marzo 1493* [Columbus's Letter Announcing the Discovery of the New World, 15 February — 14 March 1493] (Madrid, 1956), 20.

5. Ezequiel Martínez Estrada, "El Nuevo Mundo, la Isla de Utopía y la Isla de Cuba" [The New

World, the Island of Utopia, and the Island of Cuba], *Casa de las Américas* 33 (November–December 1965); this issue is entitled *Homenaje a Ezequeil Martínez Estrada.*

6. *The Complete Essays of Montaigne,* trans. Donald Frame (Stanford, Calif., 1965), 152.

7. Ibid.

8. In William Shakespeare, *Obras completas,* trans. Luis Astrana Marín (Madrid, 1961), 107–8.

9. For example, Jan Kott notes that "there have been learned shakespearian scholars who tried to interpret *The Tempest* as a direct autobiography, or as an allegorical political drama" (*Shakespeare, Our Contemporary,* trans. Boleslaw Taborski, 2d ed. (London, 1967), 240.

10. Ernest Renan, *Caliban: Suite de "La Tempête." Drame Philosophique* [Caliban: "The Tempest" Suite. A philosophical Drama] (Paris, 1878).

11. See V. Arthur Adamov. *La Commune de Paris (8 mars–28 mars 1871): Anthologie* [The Paris Commune (8 March–28 March 1871): An Anthology] (Paris, 1959); and, especially, Paul Lidsky, *Les écrivains contre la Commune* [Writers Against the Commune] (Paris, 1970).

12. Lidsky, Paul, *Les écrivains contre la Commune,* 82.

13. Cited by Aimé Césire in *Discours sur le colonialisme* [An Address on Colonialism], 3d ed. (Paris 1955), 13. This is a remarkable work, and I have made extensive use of its main ideas in this essay. (A part of it has been translated into Spanish in *Casa de las Américas* 36–37 [May–August 1966], an issue dedicated to *Africa en América* [Africa in Latin America]).

14. Ibid., 14–15.

15. See Roberto Fernández Retamar, "Modernismo, noventiocho, subdesarrollo" [Modernism, the Generation of 1898, Underdevelopment], paper read at the Third Congress of the International Association of Hispanists, Mexico City, August 1968; collected in *Ensayo de otro mundo* [Essay on a Different World], 2d ed. (Santiago, 1969).

16. Quoted in José Enrique Rodó, *Obras completas* [Complete Works], ed. Emir Rodríguez Monegal (Madrid, 1957), 193; this volume will hereafter be cited by page number in the text.

17. See Jean Franco, *The Modern Culture of Latin America: Society and the Artist* (London, 1967), 49.

18. José Vasconcelos, *Indología* [Indology], 2d ed. (Barcelona, n.d.), XXIII.

19. Mario Benedetti, *Genio y figura de José Enrique Rodó* [A Portrait of José Enriqué Rodó] (Buenos Aires, 1966), 95.

20. The penetrating but negative vision of Jan Kott causes him to be irritated by this fact. "Renan saw Demos in Caliban; in his continuation of *The Tempest* he took him to Milan and made him attempt another, victorious coup against Prospero. Guéhenno wrote an apology for Caliban-People. Both these interpretations are flat and do not do justice to Shakespeare's Caliban" (*Shakespeare, Our Contemporary,* 273).

21. Guéhenno's weakness in approaching this theme with any profundity is apparent from his increasingly contradictory prefaces to successive editions of the book (2d ed., 1945; 3d ed., 1962) down to his book of essays *Calibán et Próspero* [Caliban and Prospero] (Paris, 1969), where according to one critic, Guéhenno is converted into "a personage of bourgeois society and beneficiary of its culture," who judges Prospero "more equitably than in the days of *Calibán parle*" (Pierre Henri Simon, in *Le Monde,* 5 July, 1969).

22. See Michael Lowy, *La pensée de Che Guevara* [Che Guevara's Thought] (Paris, 1970), 19.

23. Aníbal Ponce, *Humanismo burgués y humanismo proletario* [Bourgeois Humanism and Proletarian Humanism] (Havana, 1962), 83.

24. J. L. Zimmerman, *Países pobres, países ricos: La brecha que se ensancha* [Poor Countries, Rich Countries: The Breech that is Widening], trans. G. González Aramburo (Mexico City, 1966), 7.

25. O. Mannoni, *Psychologie de la colonisation* [The Psychology of Colonialism] (Paris, 1950), 71; quoted by Frantz Fanon, in *Peau noire, masques blancs* [Black Skin, White Masks], 2d ed. (Paris [c. 1965]), 106.

26. George Lamming, *The Pleasured of Exile* (London, 1960), 109. In commenting on these opinions of Lamming, the German Janheinz Jahn observes their limitations and proposes an identification of Caliban/negritude (see *Neo-African Literature*, trans. O. Coburn and U. Lehrburger [New York, 1968], 239–42).

27. John Wain, *the Living World of Shakespeare* (New York, 1964), 226–27.

28. See Aimé Césaire, *Une tempête: Adaptation de "La Tempête" de Shakespeare pour un théâtre nègre* [A Tempest: An Adaptation of Shakespeare's "The Tempest" for a Black Theater] (Paris, 1969); Edward Brathwaite, *Islands* (London, 1969); Roberto Fernández Retamar, "Cuba hasta Fidel" [Cuba until Fidel], *Bohemia*, 19 September 1969.

29. The new reading of *The Tempest* has become a common one throughout the colonial world of today. I want only, therefore, to mention a few examples. On concluding these notes, I find a new one in the essay by James Ngugi (of Kenya), "Africa y la descolonizatión cultural" [Africa and Cultural Decolonization], in *El correo* (January 1971).

30. "It is improper," Benedetti has said, "to confront Rodó with present-day structures, statements, and ideologies. His time was different from ours[;] . . . his true place, his true temporal homeland was the nineteenth century" (*Genio y figura de José Enrique Rodó*, 128).

31. Ibid., 109. Even greater emphasis on the current validity of Rodó will be found in Arturo Ardao's book *Rodó: Su americanismo* [Rodó: His Americanism] (Montevideo, 1970), which includes an excellent anthology of the author of *Ariel*. On the other hand, as early as 1928, José Carlos Mariátegui, after rightly recalling that "only a socialist Latin or Ibero-America can effectively oppose a capitalist, plutocratic, and imperialist North America," adds, "The myth of Rodó has not yet acted — nor has it ever acted — usefully and fruitfully upon our souls" ("Aniversario y balance" [An Anniversary and a Summing Up] [1928], in *Ideología y política* [Ideology and Politics] [Lima, 1969], 248).

32. *Hombres de la revolucion: Julio Antonio Mella* [Men of the Revolution: Julio Antonio Mella] (Havana, 1971), 12.

33. Ibid., 15.

34. See Erasmo Dumpierre, *Mella* (Havana, c. 1965), 145; see also José Antonio Portunondo, "Mella y los intelectuales" [Mella and the Intellectuals] [1963], which is reproduced in *Casa de las Américas*, no. 68 (1971).

35. Emir Rodríguez Monegal, ed., *Rodó* (Madrid, 1957), 193–93; my emphasis.

36. Medardo Vitier, *Del ensayo americano* [On the Latin-American Essay] (Mexico City, 1945), 117.

37. Fidel Castro, speech, 19 April 1971.

38. See Kott, *Shakespeare, Our Contemporary*, 269.

39. See Ezequiel Martínez Estrada, "Por una alta cultural popular y socialista cubana" [Toward a Cuban Popular and Socialist High Culture] [1962], in *En Cuba y al servicio de la Revolución cubana* [In Cuba and at the Service of the Cuban Revolution] (Havana, 1963); "Martí en su (tercer) mundo" [Martí in his (Third) World] [1964], in *Ensayo de otro mundo, Cuba Socialista* 41 (January 1965); Noël Salomon, "José Martí et la prise de conscience latinoaméricaine" [José Martí and Latin America's Coming to Consciousness], *Cuba Sí* 35–36 (4th trimester 1970–1st trimester 1971); and Leonardo Acosta, "La concepción histórica de Martí," [Martí's Idea of History], *Casa de las Américas* 67 (July–August 1971).

40. Pedro Henríquez Ureña, *Obra crítica* [Critical Work] (Mexico City, 1960), 27.

41. Ivan Schulman (*Martí, Casal y el modernismo* [Martí, Casal, and Modernism] [Havana, 1969] 92) has discoverd that it had been *previously* published on 10 January 1891, in *La Revista Illustrada de Nueva York*.

42. Manuel Pedro González, "Evolución de la estimativa martiana" [The Evolution of Martí's Critical Tools], in *Antología crítica de José Martí* [Critical Anthology of José Martí], comp. and ed. Manuel Pedro González (Mexico City, 1960), xxix.

43. Nonetheless, this should not be understood to mean that I am suggesting that those authors who have not been born in the colonies should not be read. Such a stupidity is untenable. How could we propose to ignore Homer, Dante, Cervantes, Shakespeare, Whitman, to say nothing of Marx, Engels, or Lenin? How can we forget that even in our own day there are *Latin American* thinkers who have not been born here? Lastly, how can we defend intellectual Robinson Crusoism at all without falling into the greatest absurdity?

44. José Martí, "Autores aborígenes americanos" [1884], in *Obras completa,* 8:336–37; hereafter cited as "AAA" in the text.

45. For instance, to Tamanaco he dedicated a beautiful poem, "Tamanaco of the Plumed Crown," in *Obras completas,* 22:237.

46. José Martí, "Fragmentos" [Frangments] [1885–95], in *Obras completas,* 22:27.

47. Ibid., 28–29.

48. See, for example, José Martí, "Mi raza" [My Race] in *Obras completas,* 2:298–300, where we read:

> An individual has no special right because he belongs to one race or another: to speak of a human being is to speak of all rights. . . . If one says that in the black there is no aboriginal fault or virus that incapacitates him from leading his human life to the full, one is speaking the truth . . . , and if this defense of nature is called racism, the name does not matter; for it is nothing if not natural decency and the voice crying from the breast of the human being for the peace and life of the country. If it be alleged that the condition of slavery does not suggest any inferiority of the enslaved race, since white Gauls with blue eyes and golden hair were sold as slaves with iron rings around their necks in the markets of Rome, that is good racism because it is pure justice and helps to remove the prejudices of the ignorant white man. But there righteous racism ends.

And, further on, "A human being is more than white, more than mulatto, more than black. Cuban is more than white, more than mulatto, more than black." Some of these questions are treated in Juliette Oullion's paper, "La discriminación racial en los Estados Unidos vista por José Martí," [Racial Discrimination in the United Staes as seen by José Martí], *Anuario martiano* (Havana, 1971), which I was unable to use, since it appeared after these notes were completed.

49. See *Casa de las Américas* 36–37 (May–august 1966), a special issue entitled *Africa en América* [Africa in Latin America].

50. I refer to the dialogue within Latin America itself. the despicable opinion that America earned in Europe's eyes can be followed in some detail in Antonello Gerbi's vast work, *La disputa del Nuevo Mundo: Historia de una polémica, 1750–1900* [The Dispute over the New World: The History of a Polemic, 1750–1900], trans. Antonio Alatorre (Mexico City, 1960).

51. José Martí, "Una Distribución de diplomas en un colegio de los Estados Unidos" [Graduation Day at a School in the United States] [1884], in *Obras completas,* 7:442.

52. Retamar, *Ensayo de otro mundo* (see n. 15 above), 15.

53. "Sarmiento, the real founder of the Republic of Argentina," Martí says of him, for example, in a letter dated 7 April 1887 to Fermín Valdés Domínguez, shortly after a warm literary elogy that the Argentinean had publicly make to him (*Obras completas,* 20:325). Nevertheless, it is significant that Martí, always so mindful of Latin American values, *did not publish a single work on Sarmiento,* not even on the occasion of his death in 1888. It is difficult not to relate this silence to Martí's often reiterated criterion that silence was his way of censuring.

54. Ezequiel Martínez Estrada, "El colonialismo como realidad" [Colonialism as a Reality], *Casa de las Américas* 33 (November–December 1965): 85. These pages originally appeared in his book *Diferencias y semejanzas entre los países de la América Latina* [Differences and Similarities Among Countries of Latin America] (Mexico City, 1962) and were written in that country in 1960; that is to say, after the triumph of the Cuban Revolution, which led Martínez Estrada to make considerable restatements of his ideas. See, for example, his "Retrato de Sarmiento" [A Portrait of Sar-

miento], a lecture given at the Biblioteca Nacional de Cuba on 8 December 1961. In it he said, "A rigorous and impartial study of the political behavior of Sarmiento in government effectively verifies the fact that many of the evils characterizing the oligarchic politics of Argentina were introduced by him"; and also "He was contemptuous of the poeple, he was contemptuous of the ignorant masses, the ill-clad masses, without understanding that this is the American people" (*Revista de la Biblioteca Nacional* (July–September 1965): 14,16.

55. Jaime Alazraki, "El indigenismo de Martí y el antindigenismo de Sarmiento" [Martí's Indigenism and Sarmiento's anti-Indigenism], *Cuadernos Americanos* (May–June 1965). The conclusion of this essay—and almost the same quotations—appear in the work of Antonio Sacoto, "El indio en la obra literaria de Sarmiento y Martí" [The Indian in the Literary Work of Sarmiento and Martí], *Cuadernos Americanos* (January–February 1968).

56. José Martí, "La verdad sobre los Estados Unidos" [The Truth about the United States], in *Páginas escogidas* [Selected Pages], ed. Roberto Fernández Retamar (Havana, 1971), 1:392.

57. Ibid., 149.

58. Domingo Faustino Sarmiento, *Páginas literarias* [Literary Pages], vol. 46 of *Obras completas* [Complete Works] (Santiago–Buenos Aires, 1885–1902), 166–73.

59. Emeterio S. Santovenia, *Genio y acción: Sarmiento y Martí* [Genius and Action: Sarmiento and Martí] (Havana, 1938), 73.

60. Jorge Luis Borges, *El tamaño de mi esperanza* [The Size of my Hope] (Buenos Aires, 1926), 5, 6.

61. On the ideological evolution of Borges with respect to his class attitudes, see Eduardo López-Morales, "Encuentro con un destino sudamericano" [An Encounter with a South American Destiny], in *Recopilación de textos sobre los vanguardismos en la America Latina* [A Collection of Texts on Latin-American Avant-Gardes], ed. Oscar Collazos (Havana, 1970); and, for a Marxist approach to the author, see Jaime Mejía Duque, "De nuevo Jorge Luis Borges" [Jorge Luis Borges Once Again], in *Literatura y realidad* [Literature and Reality] (Medellín, 1969).

62. Jorge Luis Borges, "El escritor argentino y la tradición" [The Argentine Writer and Tradition], *Sur* 232 (January–February 1955): 7.

63. José Carlos Mariátegui, "Aniversario y balance" [An Anniversary and a Summing Up], in *Ideología y política* [Ideology and Politics] (Lima, 1969), 248.

64. Jean-Jacques Servan-Schreiber, *El desafío americano* [The American Challenge] (Havana, 1968), 41.

65. Carlos Fuentes, *La muerte de Artemio Cruz* [The Death of Artemio Cruz] (Mexico City, 1962), 27.

66. No one has preserved a copy of the manifesto. There does exist, however, a copy of the article in which Ezequiel Martínez Estrada responded to it: "Réplica a una declaración intemperante" [Reply to an Intemperate Statement], in *En Cuba y al servicio de la Revolución cubana.*

67. I have dealt further with this point in "Intercomunicación y nueva literatura" [Intercommunication and New Literature], in *América Latina en su literatura* [Latin America in Its Literature], ed. César Fernández Moreno (Mexico City, 1972).

68. Carlos Fuentes, *La neuva novela hispanoamericana* [The new Latin American novel] (Mexico City, 1969), 10; hereafter cited by page number in the text.

69. Tzvetan Todorov, "Formalistes et futuristes"[Formalists and Futurists], *Tel Quel* 30 (1968): 43. And see Krystina Pomorska, *Russian Formalist Theory and Its Poetic Ambiance* (The Hague, 1968).

70. Carlos-Peregrín Otero, *Introducción a la lingüistica transformacional* [Introduction to Transformational Linguistics] (Mexico City, 1970), 1.

71. Ambrosio Fornet's analysis of the publication, in *"New World en español"* [*New World* in Spanish], *Casa de las Américas* 40 (January–February 1967), has lost none of its validity.

72. Vilfredo Pareto, *Trattato di sociologia generale* [Treatise on General Sociology] (Florence, 1916); cited in José Carlos Mariátegui, *Ideología y política*, 24.

73. Alfonso Reyes, "Notas sobre la inteligencia americana" [Notes on the Latin America Intelligentsia], in *Obras completas* [Complete Works] (Mexico City, 1960), 11:88n.

74. Ibid., 90.

75. José Martí, "Cuaderno de apuntes—5" [Notebook—5] [1881], in *Obras completas*, 21: 164.

76. Ezequiel Martínez Estrada, "El colonialismo como realidad" (see n. 54 above), 85.

77. José Carlos Mariátegui, *Siete ensayos de interpretación de la realidad peruana* [Seven Interpretative Essays on Peruvian Reality] (Havana, 1964), xii.

78. "Intellectual" in the broad sense of the word, as employed by Gramsci in his classic pages on the subject, to which I heartily subscribe. As they are sufficiently known, I do not feel it necessary to comment on them here; see Antonio Gramsci, "The Intellectuals," in *Selections from the Prison Notebooks,* ed. and trans. Quintin Hoare and Geoffrey Smith (New York, 1971). In the preparatory seminar for the Cultural Congress of Havana, 1967, the word was used by us in this same broad sense and, recently, Fidel has taken up the question again in the first National Congress on Education and Culture. There he rejected the notion that such a denomination be enjoyed by a small group of "witch doctors" that "has monopolized the title of intellectual," to the exclusion of "teachers, engineers, technicians, researchers . . . "

79. Karl Marx and Fredrick Engels, *The Communist Manifesto* (New York, 1948), 20.

80. We would do well to recall here that more than forty years ago Mariátegui wrote, "this is a moment in our history when it is not possible, in effect, to be nationalist and revolutionary without also being socialist" (*Siete ensayos,* 26n).

81. For a more recent discussion of this with respect to writers, see, in particular, Mario Benedetti, "Las prioridades del escritor" [The Writer's Priorities] *Casa de las Américas* 68 (September–October 1971).

82. Mariátegui, "Aniversario y balance" (see n. 63 above), 249.

83. See "Diez años de revolución: El intelectual y la sociedad" [Ten Years of Revolution: The Intellectual and Society], *Casa de las Américas* 56 (September–October 1969); also published under the title *El intelectual y la sociedad* [The Intellectual and Society] (Mexico City, 1969).

84. Fidel Castro, *Palabras a los intelectuales* [Words to the Intellectuals] (Havana, 1961), 5.

85. Although a certain narrow conception of socialist realism—which Che rejects in his article along with the phony vanguardism attributed to capitalist art today and its negative influence among us—has not damaged our art in the way he suggested, some harm has been done by an extemporaneous fear of the conception. The process has been described thus: For ten years Cuban novelists eluded skillfully the dangers of a narrative that would lead to schematism and paralysis. On the other hand, the greater portion of their works evince an air of timidity from which poetry and documentary film, for example, have freed themselves (and from which the writer of short stories will perhaps free himself). . . . [I]f the new narrative, given the climate of artistic freedom in which it developed, had passed through an epic phase of ingenuous exaltation of reality, perhaps it might have discovered at least its own *tone,* which would have demanded in turn the discovery of new forms. That way we would be able to discuss today, in a manner of speaking, epic vanguardism in the Cuban narrative. . . . The danger should have been incurred *proceeding from* a fall, instead of attempting to avoid one, for the fact that one does not *fall* into pamphletism does not guarantee that he will escape mimetism and mediocrity. [Ambrosio Fornet, "A propósito de Sacchario" [On Sacchario] *Casa de las Américas* 64 (January–February 1971)]

86. Ernesto Che Guevara, "Que la universidad se pinte de negro, de mulato, de obrero, de campesino" [Paint the University Black, Mulatto, Worker, Peasant], in *Obras, 1957–1967* [Works, 1957–1967] (Havana 1970), 2:37–38.

Caliban Revisited

1. That he is little-read in English can be gathered from Edward W. Said's article, "Swift as Intellectual," *The World, the Text, and the Critic* (Cambridge, Mass. 1983). I can attest to the fact that in Spanish it is even more the case. I am, however, pleased to point out Beatriz Maggi's article on Swift, *"Panfleto y literatura"* [Pamphlet and Literature], in *Panfleto y literatura* [Pamphlet and Literature] (Havana, 1982), from which I took the great Irish writer's epitaph.

2. Naturally, this does not imply the slightest disdain toward children's literature; I simply wish to point out the transmutation of a work's meaning.

3. *The 60s Without Apology,* See Sohnya Sayres, Anders Stephenson, Stanley Aronowitz, and Fredric Jameson, eds., (Minneapolis, 1984).

4. See Cristopher Lasch, "The Cultural Cold War: A Short History of the Congress for Cultural Freedom," in *Towards a New Past: Dissenting Essays in American History.* ed. Barton J. Bernstein (New York, 1967).

5. See Ambrosio Fornet, *"New World* en español" [New World in Spanish], *Casa de las Américas,* 40, (January–February, 1967).

6. See Mario Vargas Llosa, *Contra viento y marea (1962–1982)* [Against Wind and Tide (1962–1982)] (Barcelona, 1983).

7. Mario Vargas Llosa, "Epitafio para un imperio cultural" [Epitaph for a Cultural Empire], *Marcha,* 27 May 1967, 31.

8. *Libre: Revista crítica trimestral del mundo de habla éspanola* [Free: A Quarterly Critical Review of the Spanish-speaking World], no. 1 (September–November [1971]); 95–96; my emphasis.

9. Julio Cortázar to Haydée Santamaría, 2 February 1972, *Casa de las Américas* 145–146 (July–October, 1984): 148, my emphasis. (The issue was in honor of our beloved Julio Cortázar on the occasion of his death.)

10. As is well known, Padilla and his wife, Belkis Cuza, are involved in an active and clownish counterrevolutionary campaign outside of Cuba. It is less well known that comrades Díaz Martínez, César López and Pablo Armando Fernández—who were accused by Padilla—live and work under normal conditions in Cuba and frequently represent the country abroad.

11. Vargas Llosa, *Contra viento y marea,* 166–67.

12. Julio Cortázar: "Apuntes al margen de una relectura de 1984" [Marginal Notations to a Rereading of 1984], in *Nicaragua tan violentamente dulce* [Nicaragua So Violently Sweet] (Barcelona, 1984), 13.

13. Vargas Llosa: *Contra viento y marea,* 166.

14. The latter two pieces were lengthened and published with the respective titles "Introducción a José Martí" [Introduction to José Martí] and "Para leer al Che" [For a Reading of Che].

15. See Roger Toumson, "Caliban/Cannibale ou les avatars d'un cannibalisme anagrammatique," in *Trois Calibans,* (Havana, 1981), 201–99. Although I do not deny the value that Toumson's research and speculations might have for other purposes, the use that Louis-Jean Calvet makes of my text in *Linguistique et colonialisme. Petit traité de glottophagie.* [Linguistics and Colonialism: A Short Treatise on Glottophagy] (Paris, 1974), 59, 223–24, is much closer to its original intent.

16. Emir Rodríguez Monegal, "Las metamorfosis de Calibán" [The Metamorphoses of Caliban], which appeared in English in the American academic journal *Diacritics* (no. 7 [1977]), and in Spanish in the Mexican political review *Vuelta.*

17. Lamming's book *The Pleasures of Exile,* a second edition of which was published in London in 1984, merits far more attention than I could give it in "Caliban."

18. See J. M. Cohen, *Jorge Luis Borges* (Edinburg, 1973), 107–9.

19. The best piece I've read on the political presuppositions of Borges's work is Julio Rodríguez-Luis's "La intención política en la obra de Borges: Hacia una visión de conjunto" [The Political Intention of Borges's Work: Toward an Overview], *Cuadernos Hispanoamericanos,* no. 361–362 (July–August 1980).

20. Jorge Alberto Manrique, "Ariel entre Próspero y Calibán," *Revista de la Universidad de México* (February–March 1972): 70.

21. These friends were, individually, John Beverley, Ambrosio Fornet, and Desiderio Navarro; my thanks to them for the information. And see Edward W. Said, *Orientalism* (New York, 1978).

Against the Black Legend

1. Ramón Menéndez Pidal, "La unidad del idioma" [The Unity of the Language] [1944], in *Castilla, la tradición, el idioma* [Castile, the Tradition, the Language], 3d ed. (Madrid, 955), 205.

2. Ibid., 192. On this question of the language, which has engendered so much nonsense on both sides of the Atlantic, see, in addition, Amado Alonso, *El problema de la lengua en América* [The Problem of Language in America] (Madrid, 1935), and *Castellano, español, idioma nacional: Historia espiritual de tres nombres* [Castilian, Spanish, National Language: The Spiritual History of Three Names] (Buenos Aires, 1943); and Angel Rosenblat, *El castellano de España y el castellano de América: Unidad y diferenciación* [Spain's Castilian and America's Castilian: Unity and Differentiation] (Caracas, 1962). Rosenblat notes in his enjoyable essay that "as against the inevitable diversity of popular and familiar speech, learned speech in Spanish America is strikingly similar to that of Spain. The similarity seems far greater than that of United States English or Brazilian Portuguese to the language of the former metropolis" (46).

3. Pierre Vilar, *Spain: A Brief History,* trans. Brian Tate (London, 1967), 36, 35.

4. Fernando Ortiz, "La 'leyenda negra' contra Fray Bartolomé" [The Black Legend Against Father Bartolomé], *Cuadernos Americanos* (September–October 1952): 146.

5. Alejandro Lipschütz, *El problema racial en la conquista de América y el mestizaje* [The Racial Problem in the Conquest of America and the Mestizo Question] (Santiago, 1963), 229.

6. Alejandro Lipschütz, *Marx y Lenin en la América Latina y los problemas indigenistas* [Marx and Lenin in Latin America and the Native American Problem] (Havana, 1974), 170–71.

7. Laurette Sejourné, *América Latina,* vol. 1, *Antiguas culturas precolombinas* [Latin America, vol. 1, Ancient Pre-Colombian Cultures], trans. Josefina Oliva de Coll (Madrid, 1971), 8–9.

8. Julio Le Riverend, "Problemas históricos de la conquista de América: Las Casas y su tiempo" [Historical Problems of the Conquest of America: Las Casas and his Times], *Casa de las Américas* 85 (July–August 1974): 4.

9. Karl Marx, "The Future of British Domination in India," in Karl Marx and Frederick Engels, *On Colonialism,* (Moscow, 1963), 97.

10. Karl Marx, "The So-called Primitive Accumulation" in *Capital* (New York, 1977), 1.8.760.

11. Quevedo, who was born in 1580, eight years before the defeat of the Invincible Armada, sensed the beginning of this process and reflected on it in his enormous, bitter, and genial work. In one of his best-known sonnets he wrote: "And it is far easier, oh Spain, in many ways, / that what you alone seized from all, / all in turn will seize from you alone," [Francisco de Quevedo y Villegas (1580–1645) was one of the greatest poets of the *Siglo de Oro,* the golden age of Spanish letters. — Translators' note.]

12. "In general, the concealed slavery of wage workers in Europe required, as a prop, slavery *sans phrase* — in the New World." (Marx, "The So-called Primitive Accumulation,") in *Capital,* 1.8.760.

13. See Julián Juderías, *La leyenda negra: Estudios acerca del concepto de España en el extranjero* [The Black Legend. Studies on Foreign Countries' Idea of Spain] (Madrid, 1914), and *Historia de la leyenda negra hispanoamericana* [History of the Spanish-American Black Legend] (Madrid, 1944), by the Argentinian Rómulo D. Carbia. It is not by chance that right-wing extremists in Spain and many foreign reactionaries have yielded to this "defense" of Spain with the same zeal they usually employ to justify more "modern" depredations.

14. Lenin wrote in his *Critical Remarks on the National Question* (1913):

The *elements* of democratic and socialist culture are present, if only in rudimentary form, in *every* national culture, since in *every* nation there are toiling and exploited masses, whose conditions of life inevitably give rise to the ideology of democracy and socialism. But *every* nation also possesses a bourgeois culture (and most nations a reactionary and clerical culture as well) in the form, not merely of "elements," but of the *dominant* culture. Therefore, the general "national culture" *is* the culture of the landlords, the clergy and the bourgeoisie. [In *Collected Works* (Moscow, 1964), 20:24]

15. During the early years of the October Revolution and against the Proletkult's intention to pass over or reject prerevolutionary culture in toto and create a new "proletarian" culture, Lenin reiterated that "this proletarian culture can only be created knowing precisely the culture created by the whole of humanity during the course of its development and transforming it. . . . Proletarian culture has to be the logical development of the storehouse of knowledge conquered by humanity under the yoke of capitalist society, of landowning society, and of bureaucratic society. All of these roads and paths have led and continue to lead to the proletarian culture" ("Tasks of the Communist Youth Leagues," 1920). These ideas are repeated and extended in, for example, Lenin's essay "On Proletarian Culture" of the same year; in general, they provided guidance on questions of culture for the gigantic Leninist task of founding the first socialist state.

16. From the viewpoint of a liberal, Fidelino de Figueiredo wrote on this question of the "two Spains"—one of the Right, the other of the Left—in his book *As duas Espanhas* (1932; Lisbon, 1936).

17. E. G. Walter Rodney, *How Europe Under-developed Africa*, 2d ed. (London and Dar-es-Salaam, 1973).

18. Américo Castro, *España en su historia: Cristianos, moros, y judíos* [Spain in Its History: Christians, Moors, and Jews] (Buenos Aires, 1948), 14–15.

19. Ramón Menéndez Pidal, *España, eslabon entre la cristiandad y el Islam* [Spain, the Link between Christendom and Islam] (Madrid, 1956).

20. Miguel Asín Palacios, *Dante y el Islam* [Dante and Islam] (Madrid, 1927), 16.

21. José Luciano Franco, "Transculturación afrohispánica" [Afro-Hispanic Transculturation], *Santiago* 17 (March 1975): 50–56. See also on this point Fernando Henriques, "The European Image of the Non-European," in *Children of Caliban* (London, 1974), esp. 14, 15.

22. Bolívar was conscious of this fact: "Spain itself, by virtue of its African blood, its institutions, its character, ceases to be European," he told the Congress of Angostura in 1819. Far from offending, such a fact contributed to the American originality he was to proclaim proudly four years later: "We are humankind in miniature." In addition, it is well known how much "the Arab element" of Spanish culture attracted Martí. Spain's *otherness* or heterodoxy, has always interested the great creators of our America.

23. "The history of early Christianity has notable points of resemblance with the modern working-class movement." To Anton Menger's question of why socialism did not follow the fall of the Roman Empire in the West, Engels replies that "this 'socialism' did in fact, as far as it was possible at the time, exist and even became dominant—in Christianity. Only this Christianity, as was bound to be the case in the historical conditions, did not want to accomplish a social transformation in this world, but beyond it, in heaven, in eternal life after death, in the impending 'millennium.'" (Frederick Engels, "On the History of Early Christianity," in Karl Marx and Frederick Engels, *On Religion*. [New York, 1969], 316–17. See also his preface to Marx's *Class Struggles in France*).

24. Vilar, *Spain* (see n. 3 above), 44.

25. Jacques Arnault, *Historia del colonialismo* [History of Colonialism], trans. Raúl Sciarreta (Buenos Aires, 1960) 10; originally published as *Procès du Colonialisme* (Paris, 1958).

26 "Entrevista con Jean-Paul Sartre" [Interview with Jean-Paul Sartre] in *Libre* 4 (1974), 10. Note that this publication, whose subtitle was *A Quarterly Critical Review of the Spanish-Speaking World,* let this remark pass without the slightest criticism or comment.

27. Jean-Jacques Fol, "Notes de lecture" [Critical Notes], *Europe* (January–February 1974): 286.

28. Manuel Galich, "El indio y el negro, ahora y antes" [Indians and blacks, Then and Now], *Casa de las Américas* 36–37 (May-August 1966), a special issue on *Africa in America*.

29. Fernando Ortiz, prologue to José Antonio Saco, *Historia de la esclavitud de la raza africana en el Nuevo Mundo y en especial en los paises américo-hispanos* [History of Black Slavery in the New World and Especially in the Countries of Spanish America] (Havana, 1938), 1:lix.

30. See Ortiz, "La 'leyenda negra'" (n. 4 above); see also Silvio Zavala, ¿Las Casas, esclavista?" [Las Casas, a Slaveholder?], *Cuadernos Americanos* (March–April 1944) and Juan Comas, "Fray Bartolomé, la esclavitud y el racismo" [Father Bartolomé, Slavery and Racism], *Cuadernos Americanos* (March–April 1976).

31. Ortiz, "La 'leyenda negra,' " 183–84.

32. Unfortunately, Menzéndez Pidal has also repeatedly contributed to this anti-Las Casas legend in " '¿Codicia insaciable?' '¿Ilustres hazañas?' " [Insatiable Greed? Illustrious Deeds?] (1940), in *La lengua de Cristóbal Colón: El estilo de Santa Teresa y otro estudios del siglo XVI* [The Language of Christopher Columbus. Saint Theresa's Style and Other Studies on the Sixteenth Century] (Buenos Aires, 1942); "Vitoria y Las Casas" [Vitoria and Las Casas], (1956), and "Una norma anormal del Padre Las Casas" [An Abnormal Norm of Father Las Casas] in *El Padre Las Casas y la leyenda negra* [Father Las Casas and the Black Legend] (Madrid, 1958); and *El padre Las Casas: su doble personalidad* [Father Las Casas: His Dual Personality] (Madrid 1963); Menéndez Pidal compares Las Casas negatively to Bernal Díaz and Vitoria, and wildly accuses him of slander and of having "established, intensified and perpetuated the Black Legend" (*El padre Las Casas y la leyenda negra,* p. 11), and states that he was anti-black, a slaver, and, finally . . . paranoid. Lipschütz responded to the latter charge in "La paranoia y el histerismo de los profetas" [Paranoia and the Hysteria of the Prophets], *Marx and Lenin en la América Latina,* see n. 6. On this and other historical points, the eminent philologist, otherwise the very soul of objectivity, proves to be the heir of another great Spanish fanatic and polymath, Marcelino Menéndez y Pelayo. The latter's sadly reactionary criteria do not, however, invalidate his enormous work which, despite its author's ideology, should not be left in the hands of Spanish reactionaries. It is still an arsenal of the most varied thoughts. An attempt to distinguish between what is alive and what is dead in that great oeuvre was made by Guillermo de Torre in *Menéndez y Pelayo y las dos Españas* (Buenos Aires, 1943) (unfortunately, a rather poor attempt, due to the habitual superficiality of its author). After reading this little book, one is convinced of the importance of doing a more serious job on this matter.

33. See for example, J. Vincens Vives, ed., *Historia de España y América* [History of Spain and Latin America] (Barcelona, 1961), especially 3:250–386; and Le Riverend, "Problemas históricos de la conquista de América" [Historical Problems of the Conquest of America] (see n. 8 above).

34. Vilar, *Spain,* 27, 39, 46, 47.

35. In his spiritedly bookish youth, Menéndez Pelayo tried to deny this fact (see *La ciencia española* [Spanish Science] [1876]). But in 1894 he already recognized the decadent state of Spanish science of his time ("Esplendor y decadencia de la cultura científica española" [The Splendor and Decadence of Spanish Scientific Culture], in *Antología del pensamiento de lengua española en la Edad Contemporánea* [Anthology of Contemporary Thought in the Spanish-speaking World], ed. José Gaos [Mexico City, 1945]). For his part, Santiago Ramón y Cajal, with the authority given to him by his great scientific work on the international level, affirms that the output of Spanish science, judged globally, "has been poor and discontinuous, visibly backward in comparison to the rest of Europe, and, especially, of a deplorable theoretical wretchedness" ("Nuestro altraso cultural y sus causas pretendidas" [Our Cultural Backwardness and its Supposed Causes], in *El concepto contemporáneo de España: Antologia de ensayos (1895–1931)* [The Contemporary Concept of Spain: An Anthology of Essays (1985–1931)], ed. Angel del Río and M. J. Benardete [Buenos Aires, 1946], 46).

36. Manuel Tuñón de Lara, *La España del siglo XIX* [Nineteenth-century Spain], 4th ed. (Barcelona, 1973), 10.

37. Roberto Mesa, *El colonialismo en la crisis del siglo XIX español* [Colonialism in the Crisis of Nineteenth-century Spain] (Madrid, 1967), 12–13.

38. In the Gaos *Antología* (see n. 35 above) there is a good overview of thought on Spain's decadence and the independence movement in America.

39. Karl Marx, "Revolutionary Spain," written for the *New York Daily Tribune*, 9 September 1854.

40. Roberto Mesa, "Prólogo a la edición española" [Prologue to the Spanish Edition], in *El anticolonialismo europeo desde Las Casas a Marx* [European Anticolonialism from Las Casas to Marx], ed. Marcel Merle and Roberto Mesa (Madrid, 1972), 8. As high representatives of that "moment," we must also mention the chroniclers of Indian cultures like Sahagún (*Cronistas de las culturas precolombinas* [Chroniclers of pre-Columbian Cultures], comp. and ed. Luis Nicolau d'Olwer [Mexico City, 1963]).

41. See Marcel Bataillon's outstanding *Erasmo y España: Estudios sobre la historia española del siglo XVI* [Erasmus and Spain: Studies on sixteenth-century Spanish history], trans. Antonio Alatorre (Mexico City, 1950), especially the appendix, "Erasmo y el Nuevo Mundo" [Erasmus and the New World], 2: 435–54.

42. See Juan López Morillas, *El krausimsmo español: Perfil de una aventura intelectual* [Spanish Krausism: Profile of an Intellectual Adventure] (Mexico City, 1956). Arturo Andrés Roig has provided an example for scholars in other Spanish-American countries with his book *Los krausistas argentinos* [The Argentine Krausists] (Puebla, 1969).

43. Carlos Blanco Aguinaga has studied in a useful book, *Juventud del 98* [The Youth of the Generation of 1898] (Madrid, 1970), how the writers grouped under the label "the Generation of '98" approached "the problem of Spain" between 1890 and 1905 from radical sociopolitical prospects that went from intransigent federalism to Marxism (xii) and how in their capacity as petty-bourgeois intellectuals "acabaron volviendo, cada uno en su modo, a recogerse en el seno de la sociedad establecida" ["ended up returning, each in his own way, to take refuge in the bosom of established society"] (326).

44. We do not mention Portugal here, despite its known contributions to world art and literature, because that country has suffered the lash of the anti-Spanish Black Legend, a legend with a definite anti-Iberian form. Of course, we must not forget that "Portugal is not a Spanish problem, and it is as alien and as close to greater Spain as Poland is to Russia, Belgium to France. . . . It is not part of either of the two Spains" (Fidelino de Figueiredo, *Las dos Españas* [see n. 16 above], 271, 276). The Black Legend has affected other peoples of the Iberian Peninsula, the Basque, Galician, Catalan, even more strongly. They were oppressed by a reactionary Castilian Spain, against which they have never tired of fighting in search of a just federal solution.

45. Juan Marinello, "Sobre Martí escritor: La expañolidad literaria de José Martí" [On Martí the writer: The literary Spanishness of José Martí], in *Vida y pensamiento de Martí: Homenaje a la ciudad de La Habana en el cincuentenario de la fundación del Partido Revolucionario Cubano, 1892–1942* [The Life and Thought of Martí: Homage to the City of Havana on the Fiftieth Anniversary of the Foundation of the Cuban Revolutionary Party, 1892–1942] (Havana, 1942). Guillermo Díaz-Plaja could affirm of Martí, that he is a "gigantic phenomenon of the Hispanic language, strong root of Ruben Dario's prose, and, without doubt, the first 'creator' of prose in the Hispanic world" (*Modernismo frente a noventa y ocho: Una introducción a la literatura española del siglo XX* [Modernism versus the Generation of 1898: An Introduction to Twentieth-century Spanish Literature] [Madrid, 1951], 305).

46. Mirta Aguirre, *La obra narrativa de Cervantes* [The Narrative Work of Cervantes] (Havana, 1971).

47. Federico de Onís, "La eternidad de España en America" [The Eternal Meaning of Spain in America], in *España en America* [Spain in America] (San Juan, 1968), 190.

Some Theoretical Problems of Spanish American Literature

1. Kurt Schnelle, "Acerca del problema de la novela latinoamericana" [Concerning the problem of the Latin-American Novel], in Kurt Schnelle et al., *El ensayo y la crítica literaria en Iberoamérica* [The Essay and Literary Criticism in Ibero-America] (Toronto, 1970), 162.

2. Ibid., 163.

3. Mario Benedetti: "La palabra, esa nueva cartuja" [Language, the New Carthusian] in *Crítica cómplice* [Complicitous Criticism] (Havana, 1971), 36, 37. These concepts can be found in other works by Benedetti.

4. See, for example, Roberto Fernández Retamar, *Ensayo de otro mundo* [Essay on Another World] (Havana, 1967; 2d rev. ed., Santiago, 1969); "Diez años de revolución: el intelectual y la sociedad" [Ten years of Revolution: The Intellectuals and Society], *Casa de las Américas* 56 (September–October 1969), and separately in Mexico, 1969; and "Calibán" [Caliban] *Casa de las Américas* 68 (September–October 1971), and separately in several editions.

5. See, especially, Roberto Fernández Retamar, "Para una teoría de la literatura hispanoamericana" [Notes Toward a Theory of Spanish-American Literature], in *"Para una teoría de la literatura hispanoamericana" y otras aproximaciones* ["For a theory of Spanish-American Literature" and Other Essays] (Havana, 1975); and see David Maldavsy, *Teoría literaria general* [General Literary Theory] (Buenos Aires, 1974).

6. José Miguel Ibáñez, *La creacion poética* [Poetic Creation] (Santiago, 1969), 11.

7. Ibid., 13–14.

8. Rudolf Grossmann, *Historia y problemas de la literatura latinoamericana* [The History and Problems of Latin-American Literature] (Madrid, 1972), 46; hereafter cited by page number in the text.

9. See, for example, José Carlos Mariátegui, "El proceso de la literatura" [The Process of Literature], in *Siete ensayos de interpretación de la realidad peruana* [Seven Interpretive essays on Peruvian Reality] (Havana, 1963), 213–18.

10. The founders of scientific socialism cautioned energetically against the error of ignoring concrete specificities. A Soviet scholar recently has recalled:

> [I]t could be said that Karl Marx, Friedrich Engels, and Vladimir Ilyich Lenin spoke out repeatedly against the attempts to disfigure dogmatically certain postulates of scientific socialism regarding the general laws of historical development. For example, when criticizing the distinguished ideologue of Russian populism N. Mikailovsky for his false interpretation of *Capital*, Karl Marx wrote in a letter to the editor of the Russian journal *Otechestvenniye Zapiski* [Fatherland notes]: "He [Mikailovsky] feels he absolutely must metamorphose my historical sketch of the genesis of capitalism in Western Europe into a historico-philosphic theory of the general path every people is fated to tread, whatever the historical circumstances in which it finds itself, in order that it may ultimately arrive at the form of economy which ensures, together with the greatest expansion of the productive powers of social labor, the most complete development of man. But I beg his pardon. (He is both honoring and shaming me too much.)"

[Marx to the Editorial Board of the *Otechestvenniye Zapiski*, November 1877, in Karl Marx and Fredrich Engels, *Basic Writings on Politics and Philosophy*, Lewis S. Feuer (Garden City, N.Y., 1959), 440–41]

Vladimir Ilyich Lenin pointed out later that the peculiarity of the historical situation on the eve of the October Revolution "offered us the opportunity to create the fundamental requisites of civilisation in a different way from that of the West-European countries." [V. I. Lenin, "Our Revolution

(Apropos of N. Sukhanov's Notes)," in *The Lenin Anthology,* ed. Robert C. Tucker (New York, 1975), 705; Qtd. in Nodari Simonia:, "Proceso histórico del 'despertar de Oriente'" (The historical process of 'the awakening of the Orient') in the journal *Ciencias Sociales* [Social sciences] 3, no. 9 (1972): 207]

11. Antônio Cândido, "Literatura y subdesarrollo" [Literature and Underdevelopment], in *América Latina en su literatura* [Latin America in its Literature], ed. César Fernández Moreno (Mexico City, 1972), 340 342, 347. I do not think, however, that Cândido is entirely correct in stating that "our literatures (like those of North America) are, basically, branches of metropolitan literatures" (344), unless he clarifies that always equivocal arboreal metaphor "branch." It is evident that we are closely linked to those literatures, with their great creative moments: those moments *are our tradition as well.* But if Cândido's statement was true for centuries, it can no longer be held that *present-day* North American literature is a 'branch' of *present-day* English literature or that *present-day* Spanish-American literature is a "branch" of present-day Spanish literature. I understand the acute Cândido's words as a polemical challenge to intransigent secessionists.

12. Ibid., 347.

13. See Desiderio Navarro, ed., *Cultura, ideología y sociedad: Antología de estudios marxistas sobre la cultura* [Culture, Ideology, and Society: An Anthology of Marxist Studies on Culture] (Havana, 1975).

14. More recent concepts of culture from a semiotic point of view can be found in Yuri Lotman, "El problema de una tipología de la cultura" [The Problem of a Typology of Culture], and Ferruccio Rossi-Landi, "Programación social y comunicación" [Social programming and communication], both in *Casa de las Américas* 71 (March–April 1972). A vivid idea of our culture and its relations will be found in Alejo Carpentier, "De lo real maravillosamente americano" [On the (Latin) American Magically Real], in *Tientos y diferencias* [Themes and Variations] (Mexico City, 1964): this piece appears under the title "De lo real maravilloso americano" [On (Latin) American Magic Realism] in later editions (Havana, 1974, for example).

15. See Alejandro Lipschütz, *Perfil de Indoamérica de nuestro tiempo: Antología, 1937–1962* [A Profile of Indo-America in Our Time. An Anthology, 1937–1962] (Havana, 1972), 92. In that capital book, Lipschütz combats the "disdain for non-European cultural facts which is the firm basis of Europe's cultural politics in Asia, Africa, Australia, and even Latin America" (93). For Lipschütz's idea of culture, see 40.

16. Miklos Szabolsci, "L'enseignement de la littérature en Hongrie" [The Teaching of Literature in Hungary], in the collective work, *L'enseignement de la littérature* (Paris, 1971), 612–13.

17. In our case powerful *transculturations,* which have been studied by, among others, Fernando Ortiz (with regard to our African heritage) and Lipschütz (on native Americans).

18. Roberto Fernández Retamar, "Martí en su (tercer) mundo" [Martí in his (Third) World], *Cuba socialista* 41 (January 1965): 55. This essay has been republished several times; see also the companion piece, "Notas sobre Martí, Lenín y la revolución anticolonial" [Notes on Martí, Lenín, and the Anticolonial Revolution], *Casa de las Américas* 59 (March–April 1970), where I sketch a parallel between our countries and the European periphery.

19. See Vladimir Ilyich Lenin, Preparatory Notes for *Imperialism: The Highest Stage of Capitalism,* in vol. 22 of *Collected Works* (Moscow, 1964), 185–87.

20. We would need a historical study of *stadial regions* of the kind posed by the Soviet historian Alexander Chistozvonov in "Estudio de las revoluciones burguesas europeas de los siglos XVI–XVII por estadios y regiones" [The Study of European Bourgeois Revolutions of the Sixteen and Seventeenth Centuries by Stadia and Regions], *Ciencias Sociales* 4, no. 14 (1973). In it he studies "the stadial-regional form of capitalist development in Central and Eastern Europe," in whose revolutions "there also arose tasks of national liberation and apolitical tasks," and he further contends that "more complex, mediated (and, for the present, little-known) connections are typical of the 'Iberian cycle' of nineteeth-century revolutions and the revolutionary wars of liberation in the countries of

Latin America. We believe it possible to relate the latter to the stadial type during the period of man-ufactures'' (112–13).

21. See Alejandro Lipschutz, *Marx y Lenin en la América Latina y los problemas indigenistas* [Marx and Lenin in Latin America and the Problems of Indigenous Peoples] (Havana, 1974), espe-cially "Lenin y nuestros problemas latinoamericanos" [Lenin and our Latin American Problems]. In the early nineteenth century Alexander von Humboldt had already pointed out in passing that the "the political and moral state" of "the Russian empire" had "many notable points in common" with New Spain (*Ensayo político sobre el reino de la Nueva España* [A Political Essay on the Kingdom of New Spain].

22. Ulrich Weisstein, *Comparative Literature and Literary Theory* (Bloomington, Ind. 1973), 29. Broader criteria can be found in I. Soter et al., *La littérature comparée en Europe orientale: Con-férence de Budapest, 26-29 octobre 1962* [Comparative Literature in Eastern Europe: A Conference Held in Budapest, 26–29 October 1962] (Budapest, 1963); and Claude Pichois and André M. Rous-seau, *La literatura comparada* [Comparative Literature], trans. by G. Colón, (Madrid, 1969).

23. Roberto Schwartz has done a good study of the *functions* of *influences*; see "Dependencia nacional: Desplazamiento de ideologías — Sobre la cultura brasileña en el siglo XIX" [National De-pendency: The Displacement of Ideologies — On Brazilian National Culture in the Nineteenth Cen-tury], *Casa de las Américas* 81 (November–December 1973).

24. Vera Kuteishchikova, *La novela mexicana: La formación, la originalidad, la etapa contem-poránea* [The Mexican novel: The Formation, the Originality, the Contemporary Period] (in Russian) (Moscow, 1971); and in *"Valoración múltiple de la novela de la revolución Mexicana"* [A Many-Sided Evaluation of the Novel of the Mexican Revolution], forthcoming in *Casa de las Américas*.

25. Adrián Marino: "Sobre la crítica de Martí" [On Martí's criticism], *Cahiers Roumains d'études littéraires,* no. 1 (1974): 143.

26. Alfonso Reyes: *El deslinde. Prolegómenos a una teoría literaria* [The Line of Demarcation: Prolegomena to a Literary Theory] (Mexico City, 1944); all quotations are from this edition; hereafter cited as *D.* A new edition has been published in vol. 15 of Reyes's *Obras completas* [Complete Works] (Mexico City, 1963), painstakingly presented by Ernesto Mejía Sánchez, to which was ap-pended Reyes's "Apuntes para la teoría literaria" [Notes for Literary Theory]. As Mejía Sánchez states, Reyes's "literary thought" is also to be found in, at very least, vol. 14 of his *Obras completas* [Complete works] (Mexico City, 1962), and in *Al yunque, 1944–1958* [At the Forge 1944–1958], (Mexico City, 1960).

27. Reyes was a precursor in more ways than one. For example, certain distinctions that at the time seemed excessively technical may now be compared with those proposed by Galvano della Volpe in his *Critica del gusto* [Critique of Taste], 2d ed. (Milan, 1964): for instance, what Reyes called "colloquium" and "paraloquium" (*D,* 194) and what Della Volpe calls "univocal," "equivocal," "polymeaning or poliseme," (*Critica,* 121–22).

28. See an allusion to this point in Mejía Sánchez's prologue to the edition of *El deslinde* in the *Obras completas,* 15: 9. José Antonio Portuondo's review of the first edition of the book had already observed: "[I]t would be proper to point out that this kind of phenomenological analysis bears no similarity to the procedures followed by the partisans of stylistics" ("Alfonso Reyes y la teoría lite-raria" [Alfonso Reyes and Literary Theory], in *Concepto de la poesía* [The Concept of Poetry], 2d ed. [Havana, 1972], 173).

29. Roman Jakobson, "Fragments de *La nouvelle poésie russe* [Fragments of *The New Russian Poetry*], in *Questions de poétique* [Questions of Poetics], trans. Tzvetan Todorov (Paris, 1973), 15, hereafter cited as *QP.*

30. See B. Eikhenbaum, "La théorie de la 'méthode formelle,'" in *Théorie de la littérature . . . des formalistes russes* (Paris, 1965), 37. See also, in English, Eikhenbaum, "The Theory of the 'Formal Method,'" in *Russian Formalist Criticism: Four Essays,* trans. and ed. Lee T. Lemon and Marion J. Reis (Lincoln, Neb., 1965), 99–139.

31. Regarding this refusal, this defect, Krystina Pomorska writes: "But the *Opojaz* members never introduced the problem of evaluation into their system; to put it more categorically, they did not think that scholarly procedure should be an evaluative one at all. Indeed, they seem to accept silently the principle enounced by Croce: that our evaluation of art is always and necessarily intuitive," (*Readings in Russian Poetics: Formalism and Structuralist Views*, ed. Ladislav Mateyka and Krystina Pomorska [Cambridge, Mass., 1972], 275).

32. Jurij Tynjanov, "Il fatto letterario" [The Literary Fact], in *Avanguardia e tradizione* trans. Sergio Leone (Bari, 1968), 26; hereafter cited by page number in the text.

33. Jurij Tynjanov, "On Literary Evolution," in *Readings in Russian Poetics*, 69.

34. As André Gisselbrecht has pointed out. See "Marxisme et théorie de la littérature," in *Littérature et idéologies*, special issue of *La Nouvelle Critique* no. 39 (1970): 33.

35. See Roberto Fernández Retamar, "A propósito del Círculo de Praga y del estudio de nuestra literatura" [A Propos of the Prague Circle and the Study of Our Literature], in *"Para una teoría de la literatura hispanoamericana" y otras aproximaciones*, (see n. 5 above), 29–44.

36. José Antonio Portuondo, "El rasgo predominante en la novela hispanoamericana" [The Distinguishing Feature of the Spanish-American Novel] (1951), in *El heroismo intelectual* [Intellectual Heroism] (Mexico City, 1955), 106; emphasis mine.

37. José Antonio Portuondo, "Literatura y sociedad" [Literature and Society] (1969), *América Latina en su literatura* (see n. 11 above), 391; emphasis mine.

38. One of the finest students of these "novels," Adalbert Dessau, confesses that "such works [by Azuela, Guzmán, Vasconcelos, even Romero] are more like memoirs than real novels" (*La novela de la Revolución Mexicana* [The Novel of the Mexican Revolution] [Mexico City, 1972], 18.

39. H. R. Hays, "La poesía latinoamericana" [Latin-American Poetry], *Gaceta del Caribe* 1, nol. 3 (May 1944): 16.

40. Pedro Henríquez Ureña, *Literary Currents in Hispanic America* (Cambridge, Mass., 1946), 147.

41. José Martí, "Julián del Casal" in *Ensayos sobre arte y literatura* [Essays on Art and Literature], ed. Roberto Ferández Retamar (Havana, 1972), 234. In this brief text, Martí traces what would be the parabola of "modernism" (a term he does not use): "This literary generation, so like a [Latin] American family, began with decorative imitation and has gone on to free, concise elegance, and to the sincere, brief, finely wrought artistic expresssion of personal feeling and direct, truly native understanding."

42. Tomás Navarro [Tomás] *Métrica española: Reseña histórica y descriptiva* [Spanish Prosody: A Historical and Descriptive Survey] (New York, 1956), 250–51. See also the worthwhile "Panorama histórico del género [the *décima*] en España e Hispanoamerica" [A Historical Overview of the Genre (the *décima*) in Spain and Spanish America], in the notable study by Ivette Jiménez de Báez, *La décima popular en Puerto Rico*, [The Popular *décima* in Puerto Rico] (Xalapa, Veracruz [Mexico], 1964). Unfortunately, the author was unaware of Samuel Feijóo's research on the popular Cuban *décima*, see, for example, *Los trovadores del pueblo* [The People's Troubadours] (Santa Clara [Cuba], 1960), 1.

43. Carlos H. Magis, *La lírica popular contemporánea: España, México, Argentina* [Contemporary Popular Lyric Poetry: Spain, Mexico, Argentina] (Mexico City, 1969), 526. Nevertheless, Carolina Poncet (*El romance en Cuba* [The Spanish Medieval Ballad Form in Cuba] [1914; Havana, 1972]), takes the view that in the eighteenth century, Spanish popular poetry also made use of the *décima*, (20–21), and she cites in support of her argument a curious and incontrovertible passage from the French traveler J. P. Bourgoing (21 n. 20).

44. See Sócrates Nolasco, *Una provincia folklórica: Cuba, Puerto Rico, y Santo Domingo* [A Province of Folklore: Cuba, Puerto Rico, and Santo Domingo] (Santiago de Cuba, 1952), 24.

45. Poncet, *El romance en Cuba*, 13, 15, 20, 26, and see 21 n. 20.

46. In *El "Martín Fierro"* [On "Martín Fierro"] (Buenos Aires, 1953), Jorge Luis Borges cites Unamuno's view of *"Martin Fierro's* monotonous *décimas."* Borges comments: "It may not be fruitless to point out that the 'monotonous *décimas . . .* are actually *sextinas"* (71–72). It is well known that *sextinas* belong to *arte mayor* [i.e., lines of verse longer than eight syllables.—Trans. note], so Borges is equally in error. The stanza in question is a *sextilla* (see Eleuterio F. Tiscornia; *La lengua de "Martín Fierro"* [The Language of "Martín Fierro"] [Buenos Aires, 1930], 284), but of a kind so "original" ("there is no precedent for them in gaucho poetry"), that it is nothing other than a *décima* (a common enough stanza in gaucho poetry) with the first four lines removed, which leaves the fifth line (the first of the *sextilla*) unrhymed. Unamuno, then, was not quite as lost on this point as the always clever (and erronous) Borges.

47. Waldo Frank, "Notes on Alfonso Reyes," in Waldo Frank et al., *Páginas sobre Alfonso Reyes* [Pages on Alfonso Reyes] (Monterrey, 1955), I: 415.

48. Of course our countries had novels back then, and even Arturo Torres Ríoseco, reworking two previous books, brought out a work with the title *Grandes novelistas de la América hispana* [Great Novelists of Hispanic America] (Berkeley and Los Angeles, 1949). But Adalbert Dessau seems right in seeing our novels as "historical consciousnesss," when, referring to the Spanish-American novel prior to the developments of recent years, he writes:

> [T]he representative Latin American novels are rather lacking in the human dimension because, in a barely modified atmosphere of colonialism and feudalism, the authors themselves had not reached the stage in the process of individualization proper to the rise of bourgeois society . . . [M]any nineteenth-and even twentieth-century novels . . . are actually essays in the sense that, given the lack of other forms and the immaturity of the genre, something that could better have been published as a pamphlet or an essay was given a novelistic form." ["La novela latinoamericana como conciencia histórica" ("The Latin-American Novel as Historical Consciousness") in *Actas del Tercer Congreso Internacional de Hispanistas* (Proceedings of the Third International Congress of Hispanists) (Mexico City, 1970), 259.]

49. See Carpentier, *Tientos y diferencias* (see n. 14 above), especially "Problemática de la actual novela latinoamericana" [Prolematics of the Present-Day Latin-American Novel].

50. Hays, "La poesía latinoamericana," 16 n. 36.

51. Schnelle, "Acerca del problema de la novela latinoamericana" (see n. 1 above), 165–66 n. 1.

52. Dessau, *La novela de la Revolucíon Mexicana,* 266 n. 45.

53. See Lucien Goldmann, "Nouveau roman et realité" [The *Nouveau Roman* and Reality], in *Pour une sociologie du roman* [Toward a Sociology of the Novel] (Paris, 1964).

54. Rita Schober, "Périodisation et historiografie littéraire" [Periodization and Literary Historiography], in Schober et at., *Problémes de périodisation dans l'histoire littéraire: Colloque international organisé par la section d'études romanes de l'Université Charles de Prague, 29 november–1 decembre 1966* [Problems of Periodization in Literary History: International Colloquium Organized by the Section of Romance Studies of the Charles University of Prague, 29 November–1 December 1966], (Prague, 1968), 23.

55. Anatoli Lunacharski, "Tesis sobre las tareas de la crítica marxista," in *Gaceta de Cuba* 112 (May–June 1973): 27. See also, in English, Lunarcharski, "Theses on the Problems of Marxist Criticism," in *On Literature and Art,* 2d rev. ed (Moscow, 1973), 9–21.

56. Carlos Rincón, "Sobre crítica y historia de la literatura hoy en Hispanoamerica" [On Present-Day Literary Criticism and History in Spanish America], *Casa de las Américas* (September–October, 1973), 9–21.

57. For example, Raimundo Lida's essay, "Períodos y generaciones en historia literaria" [Periods and Generations in Literary History] (in *Letras hispánicas* [Hispanic Letters], [Mexico City, 1958]) comments on the symposium on periodization—limited to European literatures—held in Amsterdam in 1935. José Luis Martínez touches on these and other problems in a more "general" way in

"Problemas de historia literaria" [Problems of Literary History] (in *Problemas literarios* [Literary Problems] [Mexico City, 1955]).

58. José Antonio Portuondo, " 'Períodos' y 'generaciones' en la historiografiía literaria hispanoamericana" ['Periods' and 'Generations' in Spanish American Literary Historiography], in *La historia y las generaciones* [History and Generations] (Santiago de Cuba, 1958); hereafter cited by page number in the text.

59. See José Carlos Mariátegui, *Siete ensayos de interpretación de la realidad perauna* (see n. 9 above), 219 n. 5.

60. José Antonio Portuondo, "Esquema de las generaciones literarias cubanas" [An Overview of Cuban Literary Generations], in *La historia y las generaciones,* 104.

61. See José Antonio Portuondo, "Realidad y falacia de las generaciones" [The Reality and the Fallacy of Generations], in *La historia y las generaciones.*

62. Jan O. Fischer, "Opening Remarks," in *Problèmes de périodisation dans l'histoire littéraire* (see n. 54 above), 5. There is a serious attempt to grapple with this problem in the discriminating book by José Juan Arrom, *Examen generacional de las letras hispanoamericanas: Ensay de método* [A Generational Approach to Spanish-American Letters: An Essay on Method], 2d ed. (Bogotá, 1977).

63. Oldřich Bělič, "La Périodisation et ses problèmes" [Periodization and its Problems], in *Problèmes de périodisation dans l'histoire littéraire;* hereafter cited by page number in the text. Bělič's piece was published in Spanish in the Chilean journal *Problemas de literatura* [Literary Problems] 1, no. 2 (September 1972).

64. Zlata Potapova, "Algunos principios generales sobre la periodización en la *Historia de la literatura mundial* (sobre todo en los volúmenes consagrados a los siglos XIX y XX)" [Some General principles of periodization in the *History of World Literature* (with particular reference to the volumes on the Nineteenth and Twentieth Centuries)], in *Problèmes de périodisation dans l'histoire littéraire;* hereafter cited by page number in the text.

On the present status of what is projected to be a ten volume history, see A. Ushakov, "El Instituto Máximo Gorki de Literatura Mundial" [The Maxim Gorky World Literature Institute], *Ciencias Sociales* [Social sciences] 4, no. 6 (1971): 224.

65. I have expressed my opinion on this point in "Modernismo, noventiocho, subdesarrollo" [Modernism, the Generation of 1898, Underdevelopment], in *"Para una teoría de la literatura hispanoamericana"* y otras aproximaciones (see n. 5 above), 97–106. A critical précis of arguments through 1968 can be found in Antonio Melis, "Bilancio degli studi sul modernismo ispanoamericano" [The Present State of Studies on Spanish-American Modernism], in *Lavori della Sezione Fiorentina del Grupo Ispanistico C.N.R.* [Proceedings of the Florentine Section of the Hispanic Studies Group of the National Research Center], Seri. 2 (Florence, 1969).

66. Leonardo Acosta, "El 'barroco americano' y la ideología colonialista" [The 'American Baroque' and Colonialist Ideology] in *Unión* [Union] (September 1972): 59.

67. Federico Alvarez, "¿Romanticismo en Hispanoamerica?" [Romanticism in Spanish America?], in *Actas del Tercer Congreso Internacional de Hispanistas* (see n. 48 above), 75, 75–76.

68. Mirta Aguirre, *El romanticismo de Rousseau a Víctor Hugo* [Romanticism from Rousseau to Victor Hugo] (Havana, 1973), 413; hereafter cited by page number in the text.

69. See Noël Salomon, "José Martí et la prise de conscience latinoaméricaine" [José Martí and Latin America's coming to consciousness], in *Cuba Sí* [Cuba Yes], nos. 35–36, (4th trimester 1970–1st trimester 1971): 5–6. This important work was republished in *Anuario Martiano* [Martí Annals] 4 (Havana, 1972).

70. That need is not excluded for the simple reason that we are dealing here with something elaborated from the perspective of a class, which, as France Vernier has rightly observed, decides in each instance what literature is: not "the ensemble of literary texts" but rather "the ensemble of 'sacred' writings which, in any given period, are recognized as 'literary' by a social class"; "the dominant

class" which "tends to impose its corpus upon the dominated classes" (*Une science du littéraire est-elle possible?* [Is a Literary Science Possible?] [Paris, 1972], 4–5. The development of metropolitan bourgeoisies explains the internal coherence of the respective literary corpuses; the meager development of our dependent bourgeoisies, the chaos of our literary corpuses. In Latin America we shall never achieve that form of literary organization from a bourgeois perspective.

71. Pedro Henríquez Ureña, "Caminos de nuestra historia literaria" [Paths of our Literary History] in *Seis ensayos en busca de nuestra expresión* [Six Essays in Search of Our Own Forms of Expression], also in *Obra crítica* [Critical Works], (Mexico City, 1960), 255.

72. Camila Henríquez Ureña, (who was an adviser to the project from the outset) has given us an excellent overview of this *Colección* in "Sobre la *Colección Literatura Latinoamericana*" [On the *Colección Literatura Latinoamericana*], *Casa de las Américas* 45 (November–December 1967); for a comparison with the *Biblioteca Americana* (in the planning of which Camila Henríquez Ureña, also participated), see 160.

73. On this matter, see, for example, Jaime Mejía Duque, "El 'boom' de la narrativa latinoamericana" [The 'Boom' of Latin-American Narrative] in *Narrativa y neocoloniaje en América Latina* [Narrative and Neocolonialism in Latin America], (Bogata, 1972); and Mario Benedetti, *El escritor latinoamericano y la revolución posible* [The Latin-American Writer and the Possible Revolution] (Buenos Aires, 1974), especially 157–155.

74. Alfonso Reyes, "Fragmento sobre la interpretación social de las letras iberoamericanas" [A Fragment on the Social Interpretation of Ibero-American Letters], in *Marginalia, primera serie* [Marginalia, first series] (Mexico, 1952), 154.

75. Jaime Labastida, "Alejo Carpentier: Realidad y conocimiento estético . . . " [Alejo Carpentier: Reality and Aesthetic Knowledge . . .], in *Casa de las Américas* 87 (November–December, 1974): 24.

76. A correct way toward accomplishing that task can be found in the works of two young Cuban critics, Sergio Chaple (*Rafael María de Mendive: Definición de un poeta* [Rafael María de Mendive: Definition of a Poet] [Havana, 1973]), and Salvador Arias (*Búsqueda y análisis* [Search and Analysis] [Havana, 1974]).

77. An example of the integral criticism our literature needs is Antonio Cornejo Polar's book *Los universos narrativos de José María Arguedas* [The Narrative Universes of José María Arguedas] (Buenos Aires, 1973).

78. Jean Pérus, *Méthodes et techniques de travail en histoire littéraire* [Methods and Techniques in Literary History] (Paris, 1972), 60.

79. Vernier, *Une science du littéraire est-elle possible?*, 1. n. 67 [editorial note in *La Nouvelle Critique*, which published the essay].

80. See, for example, André Gisselbrecht, "Marxisme et théorie de la littérature" (see n. 34 above).

Prologue to Ernesto Cardenal

1. *Nueva poesía nicaragüense* [New Nicaraguan Poetry], introduction by Ernesto Cardenal, comp. and ed. Orlando Cuadra Downing (Madrid, 1949).

2. See Roberto Fernández Retamar, "Situación actual de la poesía hispanoamericana" [The present state of Spanish-American Poetry], *Revista Hispánica Moderna* 24, no. 4 (October 1958); *Para el perfil definitivo del hombre* [Toward a Definitive Profile of Man] (Havana, 1981).

3. The best of Cardenal's collections would seem to be *Poemas reunidos, 1949–1969* [Collected Poems/1949–1969], ed. Antidio Cabal (Valencia, [Venezuela], 1972). At the beginning of this book we find these words from Cardenal: "I have copied a great number of poems, I have corrected many of them, I have finished poems that had been in rough draft for years; I have disinterred a good deal of unpublished material." More up-to-date is *Poesía* [Poetry], ed. Cintio Vitier (Havana, 1979); unless expressly indicated, my citations of Cardenal are from this edition.

4. Ernesto Cardenal; "Ansias y lengua de la poesía nicaragüense" [Longings and Language in Nicaraguan Poetry], introduction to *Nueva poesía nicaragüense*, 67.

5. [Ernesto Mejía Sánchez], colophon to *"Zero Hour" and other Documentary Poems*, by Ernesto Cardenal, ed. Donald D. Walsh, trans. Paul W. Borgeson and Jonathan Cohen (1960; New York, 1980).

6. Merton states in his prologue that those poems are "a series of utterly simple poetic sketches with all the purity and sophistication that we find in the Chinese masters of the T'ang Dynasty." And he adds, "Never has the experience of novitiate life in a Cistercian monastery been rendered with such fidelity, and yet with such reserve" "Ernesto Cardenal," in *The Literary Essays of Thomas Merton*, ed. Patrick Hart (New York, 1981), 323.

7. This is José Coronel Urtecho's expression for Rubén Darío in the former's "Oda a Rubén Darío" [Ode to Rubén Darío] (1925), in *Nueva poesía nicaragüense*, 249. Mejía Sánchez also uses it in his introduction.

8. Introduction to *Epigramas* [Epigrams], by Ernesto Cardenal (Mexico City, 1961).

9. Ernesto Cardenal, "La experiencia más importante" [The Most Important Experience], *Casa de las Américas* 70 (January–February, 1972): 182. Other interviews that are of interest on this subject can be found in the Cardenal miscellany *La santidad de la revolución* [The Sanctity of the Revolution] (Salamanca, 1976).

10. Ernesto Cardenal, *In Cuba*, trans. Donald D. Walsh 1972; New York, 1974), 7.

11. Ernesto Cardenal, *The Gospel in Solintiname*, trans. Donald D. Walsh (1975; Maryknoll, N.Y., 1982).

12. Friedrich Engels, "On the History of Early Christianity," in Karl Marx and Friedrich Engels, *On Religion* (New York, 1969), 316. See also Engels's introduction to Marx's "The Class Struggles in France, 1848 to 1850," in *Marx and Engels: Basic Writings on Politics and Philosophy*, ed. Lewis S. Feuer (Garden City, N.Y., 1959), 281–317.

13. Ernesto Cardenal, "Lo que fue Solintiname (Carta al pueblo de Nicaragua)," *Casa de las Américas* num. 108 (May–June, 1978) [The Meaning of Solintiname. (A letter to the People of Nicaragua)], it has also appeared in *Nicaragua in Revolution: The Poets Speak/ Nicaragua en Revolución: Los poetas hablan—A Bilingual Collage*, ed. B. A. Aldaraca et al. (Minneapolis, 1980), 246–252.

14. See Ernesto Cardenal, "Luces" [Lights], *Casa de las Américas* 117 (November–December 1979); see also *Nicaragua in Revolution*, 284–87.

15. See Roberto Fernández Retamar, "Antipoesía y poesía conversacional en Hispanoamérica" [Antipoetry and Conversational Poetry in Spanish America] (1968) in Retamar et al., *Panorama de la actual literatura latinoamericana* [Panorama of Present-Day Latin American Literature] (Havana, 1969). See also, in Retamar, *Para el perfil* (see n. 2 above): "[T]he poetry of the person who, as I have stated several times, I consider the finest of the Spanish-American poets who follow the great figures of the avant-garde: Ernesto Cardenal" (203).

16. Juan Ramón Jiménez, "José Martí (1895)," in *Españoles de tres mundos* [Spaniards from Three Worlds], (Buenos Aires 1942), 33.

17. José Emilio Pacheco, "Nota sobre la otra vanguardia" [A Note on the Other Avant-Garde], *Casa de las Américas* 118 (January–Februrary 1980).

18. Ernesto Cardenal, qtd. in Mario Benedetti, "Ernesto Cardenal: Evangelio y revolución" [Ernesto Cardenal: Gospel and Revolution], *Casa de las Américas* 63 (November–December 1970): 175–76; rpt. in *Los poetas comunicantes* [Communicating Poets] (Montevideo, 1972), 101.

19. André Gisselbrecht, "Marxisme et théorie de la littérature' [Marxism and Literary Theory], special issue of *La Nouvelle Critique* 39 (1970): 31.

20. "The compiler of this anthology is among those who believe that literature *alone*, literature for literature's sake, is useless. Literature must be of service. This is why literature must be political.

However, not political *propaganda,* rather, political *poetry."* (Ernesto Cardenal, Introduction to *Poesía Nicaragüense,* vii).

21. Ibid., viii; and see 67.

22. Among many other writings by S. M. Eisenstein on the subject, see "The Cinematographic Principle and the Ideogram" [1929], in his *Film Form: Essay in Film Theory,* ed. and trans. Jay Leyda (New York, 1949).

23. Ariel Dorfman, "Tiempo de amor, tiempo de lucha: La unidad de los *Epigramas* de Cardenal" [A Time for Love, a Time for Struggle: The Unity of Cardenal's *Epigrams*], *Texto Crítico: Revista del Centro de Investigaciones Lingüístico-Literarias de la Universidad Veracruzana* 13, (April–June 1979): 14–15.

24. See Ernesto Cardenal, *Psalms* (1964; New York, 1981).

Index

Index

Roberto Fernández Retamar is a Cuban poet and essayist whose work has been translated into English, French, Italian, Portuguese, German and other languages. He has been a professor at the University of Havana since 1955 and is currently president of the cultural institution, Casa de las Américas, whose journal he edited between 1965 and 1988. Fernández Retamar has also been a visiting professor at Yale University. In the early 1960s he was cultural counselor of the Cuban Embassy in Paris and co-ordinating secretary of the Union of Cuban Writers and Artists, and from 1977 through 1986, director of the Martí Studies Center. Fernández Retamar's books of essays include *Idea de la estilística* (1958), *Para una teoría de la literatura hispanoamericana* (1975), *Introducción a José Martí* (1978) and *Algunos usos de civilización y barbarie* (1988), and he contributes to the journals *Cuba Socialista, Cuadernos Americanos* and *Revista de Crítica Literaria Lantinoamericana,* among others.

Edward Baker is an associate professor of Spanish at the University of Florida. He received his Ph.D. in Spanish from Harvard University. Baker has also taught at the University of California at San Diego, the University of Washington, and the University of Minnesota. He is co-editor of a collection of Nicaraguan verse, *Nicaragua in Revolution* (1980), and author of *La lira mecánica* (1986). Baker has contributed to *Revista de Occidente, Sin Nombre, VRBI,* and *Maatstaaf.*